I See Bad People

An Introduction to the Pseudopathic Leader
in Corporate America

Also by Dr. Bob

The Killing of a Nation

I See Bad People. Copyright © 2014 by Robert Allen, Ed.D. All rights reserved. Manuscript version May 4, 2014. May the forth be with you.

To my amazing wife, Tracey, sunshine of my life.

Pseu·do·path [soo-doh-path]

The word *Pseudopath* is a protologism (i.e., a prototype word) descriptive to a leader or prospective leader with a near-Pathic personality disorder. As used throughout this book, a Pathic is a "full on" Narcissist (or, Narcipath), Sociopath, or Psychopath. In layman's terms, the Pseudopath could be described as a latent Pathic. In mental-health terms, the Pseudopath would be viewed as a sub-clinical Pathic. Whatever your perspective, the Pseudopath falls just short of being clinically labeled with one or more personality disorders using diagnostic standards established by the Diagnostic and Statistical Manual of Mental Disorders (DSM). The DSM is a professional reference published by the American Psychiatric Association (APA). Webster's 2nd edition New College Dictionary assigns one definition of the word *pseudo* to be "apparently similar." Webster's also assigns one definition of the word *path* to be "one suffering from a given type of disorder <socio*path*>." So combined, *pseudo-path* occupationally describes an individual that – once in a position of dominance or authority – eventually crosses the line into Pathic behavior. The Pseudopath does not dwell in these aberrant realms, but rather, cleverly ventures in and out as opportunity permits. If you think this new word, Pseudopath, has an ominous tone to it – then very good. ***It should.***

CONTENTS

Page

Part I: Understanding the Pseudopath

Forward   2

Chapter 1. How Bad Is It?   6

    Hidden Pathosis   7
    Related Definitions   11
    Pathosis Revealed   16
    The Classic Pathic   26

Chapter 2. What Do We Know?   30

    Current Perspective   30
    Bad Leadership   32
    The Cost of Bad Leadership   36
    Pathic Leadership   41

Part II: Screening the Pseudopath

Chapter 3. Are They Worth Screening?   45

    A Virulent Pathogen Lurks   45
    A Revealing Study   49
    Overcoming Organizational Uncertainty   51

Chapter 4. Are They Even Screenable?   57

    Pathic Subtlety Testing   57
    Pathic Subtlety Investigation   62
    Investigation Factors   65
    Information Technology Factors   71
    Privacy Factors   76
    Social Factors   79
    Designing Your Screen   83

	Page
Appendix A: My Study Results	91
Appendix B: Your Screening Algorithm	120
End Notes	131
Bibliography	140

PART I

Understanding the Pseudopath

If a Psychopath is a wolf in sheep's clothing, then a Pseudopath is an adorable dog that bites without provocation.

Forward

The U.S. military offers a perfect setting for developing and nurturing leaders. In no other walk of life are leaders asked at such a young age to make such major decisions that involve billions of American dollars, or, that affect the well-being (if not the very existence) of so many people.

In 1979, aboard a nuclear-powered aircraft carrier carefully positioned in a heavily-mined gulf off the coast of an angry Persian country recently "liberated" by religious extremists, I had to make a comparatively-small decision. Command agreement had been reached to promote one of my crew into a leadership position – contrary to my every sense of good judgment, but rationalized by the insistence of my superiors. Intelligent, well spoken, and ever-confident, this particular shipmate eagerly displayed many of the outward attributes sought after in a leader – especially where an audience was involved. But this individual also had a tendency to surreptitiously venture into harmful and self-serving behaviors. This was known only to the observant few, and unfortunately, to those shipmates whom had suffered his reproachable behaviors first hand. Armed with such knowledge, however, one might question whether an individual of this sort would bring more bad than good in a leadership capacity. But rank prevailed – and I promoted him into a position of leadership. And within a few weeks, my decision had already proven itself to be a bad one.

Fast forward 30 years. Long separated from military duty and now working for a large corporation, I find myself mortified over a corporate announcement that this very individual had been an executive for numerous companies, had been recently hired by the corporation into an executive position, and would be part of a team assembled with purpose to lead performance improvements and work-culture change. My initial disbelief quickly evolved into a perplexing thought that – if history repeated itself – the disconcerting behavioral tendencies innate to this individual's character (i.e., his 'pathic fingerprint') would eventually reveal itself. This hypothesis was validated within months – and with little more than one year on the job, this leader was unceremoniously released from the company for cause (i.e., inappropriate conduct). Much to my chagrin, a regrettable leadership selection made three decades past had evolved into a series of similarly-bad decisions on the part of corporate America. In personal reflection, the ability (or inability) of a business entity to recognize pathic subtleties in leadership candidates came into question. With the national news as my informant and personal experience as my expert witness, I can only adjudge that these selection inadequacies are not uncommon across America's corporate communities. I also believe that the risks associated with these selection inadequacies are not trivial – rather, the likelihood of pseudo-paths existing within any leadership candidacy pool are high, and, the consequence of their selection can be especially damaging to both enterprise and personnel alike.

Clinical Narcissists, Sociopaths, and Psychopaths are not particularly difficult to reveal and recognize. History chronicles the harmful (and sometimes insidious) conduct of such Pathic leaders across centuries past. The word for the wise is that those whom cannot learn from history are doomed to repeat it. The subtle tendencies of the Pseudopath, on the other hand, give every appearance of being largely obscure to traditional hiring methodologies, background investigations, psychological testing, and personality profiling. Yet, from a holistic perspective, history for this ilk of leader simply cannot be ignored. The Pseudopath harbors many undesirable attributes that can foment trial and tribulation once placed into a position of authority. If unchecked or unresolved, the pseudopathic leader can drop an organization to its knees. But then – *can* we really recognize, and thus avoid, the pseudopathic leader? I'm convinced that leadership job candidates harboring (and perhaps hiding) pseudopathic tendencies can indeed be flushed-out. Twenty years ago, this might have been too difficult and costly to undertake. Today, science and technology make it both practical and cost wise. Corporate America take note! Any business entity would be so wise to recognize leadership-level Pseudopaths *before* they're hired. Because the Pseudopath is so poorly understood, it won't be easy. But it can be done.

Mental-health research and reference around the clinically diagnosable are plentiful. So those responsible for the assessment and treatment of folks with apparent behavioral or character disorders have a lot to work with. For the rest of us simple working folk – *whom are most interested in avoiding pathics altogether* – there's scant little to work with. This is unfortunate for the likes of corporate America. Pseudopaths have honed their skills of deception and manipulation over a lifetime of practice. They easily evade traditional pre-employment radar systems. They shine on paper and in the interview room, and then, venture into nefarious behaviors once in a position of authority or dominance. Corporate America is their hunting ground, and the business and its workforce become their easy prey.

I penned this book with purpose to shed some non-clinical light on the sub-clinical pathosis that is the Pseudopath. I am not in the mental health field, and I desperately want to understand the Pseudopath from an occupational perspective. There's just so little non-clinical information to draw from. And this leads me to an additional purpose for this book – to stimulate thought and concept around practical measures for recognizing Pseudopaths before they're hired. For corporate America, merely understanding the Pseudopath is not enough. Where leadership positions are involved, Corporate America would be so wise to apply pre-employment screening solutions with the Pseudopath in mind.

Chapter 1. How Bad Is It?

I'm here to tell you, it's pretty bad. Case in point. Given a need to hire a home caregiver for your children or an elderly relation, you would *certainly* want to know if any of the short-listed applicants were prone to unscrupulous behaviors. Alarmingly, the typical corporate background investigation would not root-out a Pseudopath lurking amongst the candidates you would entrust with the care of your loved ones. This revelation doesn't bode well for corporate America – because your leadership mainstream is more of a harbinger for Pseudopaths than the ordinary pool of home caregivers. Leadership is synonymous with power, and power is the perfect weapon for dominance, and dominance is the Pseudopath's trigger for self-enrichment and self-gratification. Once nestled into a position of authority, this curious character of individual is perfectly primed for pathic behavior. Their immediate victims are the workforce, in turn, eroding the workplace culture like a virulent disease. From a capitalistic perspective, the eventual result of their opportunistic psychopathy is measurable (often profound) reductions to productivity and profitability. Yet Pseudopaths abound and thrive in corporate America – and I think I know why. With a little knowledge, preparation, and adjustment to the hiring process, I also think that corporate America can keep this cancer out of the business.

Hidden Pathosis

No modern-day clinician is more studied in the field of psychopathy than Dr. Robert Hare. On the heals of Cleckley's clinical work around specific psychopathic traits during the mid 20th century, Hare created and optimized the first diagnostic test designed for the pathic sort. It is currently called the PCL-R (Revised Psychopathy Check List), and it remains the most widely applied test for assessing psychopathy. In his book, *Without Conscience: The Disturbing World of the Psychopaths Among Us*, Dr. Hare's research suggests that settings which allow for self-enrichment and self-gratification are quintessential magnets for the pathic sort. One might surmise that rigorous psychological profiling with tools such as the PCL-R or the Minnesota Multiphasic Personality Inventory (MMPI) scales would be sufficient to spot the personality disordered. And then, one might also apply custom personality-profiling tools such as the Myers-Briggs Type Indicator (MBTI) or Geier's DiSC assessment for added assurance. These additional measures of screening, however, would still fail to expose the Pseudopath. According to Drs. Schouten & Silver – perhaps the most studied of mental-health researchers in the area of subtle or latent pathosis – these types of tests were not designed with the sub-clinical pathic in mind, and as a result, can be artfully gamed.[1]

But before I begin any explanation about this "hidden" pathosis typical to Pseudopaths, I need to talk about continuums. Across the many fields of human science, continuums are pathological measuring sticks used by sociologists, psychologists, and psychiatrists (alike) that describe some manner of human nature, response, or behavior. Some continuums are categorically distinct, while others cross pathologic divisions. A Pseudopath lies in the same behavioral continuum as neurotics and psychopaths. It's easier to explain as a graph.

Figure 1: The Pathic Continuum

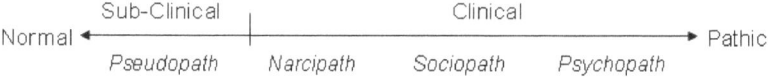

Dr. George Simon, the bestselling author of *In Sheep's Clothing: Understanding and Dealing with Manipulative People*, articulates that this particular human-character continuum "reflects how an individual deals with the challenges of life."[2] At one extreme is the severely neurotic. One might expect the opposite end to be occupied with normalcy – but it is anything but normal. Dr. Simon points out that the opposite extreme is bound by severe character disorder. Normality as it is, falls in the middle of this particular human-character continuum. Neurosis arises from conflicts between instinctual drive and conscience. Another way of looking at this is that neurotics suffer from too much conscience. Character-disorder personalities, on the other hand, are devoid of conscience when primal urges are acted upon. Another way of looking at this is that the character-disordered suffer from too little conscience. Narcissism, sociopathy, and psychopathy can be found amongst the many clinically-recognized disorders found at this end of the human-character continuum. Pseudopathy is their second cousin. And the threat to corporate America posed by the Pseudopath is greater than that posed by the full-on pathic – because the Pseudopath is cloaked in normalcy during the hiring process. Corporate America is at constant and significant risk of unknowingly hiring a Pseudopath.

But I'm wondering whether the most emphatic way to answer the question 'Just how bad is it?' is to blend results from related research conducted within America's job market. The result is an eye-opener.

Gather 100 working-age adults randomly from the general U.S. population. One psychopath is likely to be found in their midst.[3] Of the 99 ordinary Americans remaining from the sample pool of 100, three sociopaths are likely to be amongst them.[4] Of the remaining 96 ordinary Americans from the sample pool, six narcissists are likely to be included.[5] One of these narcissists will likely be of the Narcissistic Personality Disorder (NPD) type – otherwise, a narcipath (for purposes of this book). The other five are likely to be of the clinical sort that exhibit a lesser degree of narcissistic characteristics, but on a regular basis. Drs. Paul Babiak and Robert Hare, co-authors of *Snakes in Suits: When Psychopaths go to Work*, suggest that amongst a 1% pathic population, "another 10 percent or so fall into the gray zone."[6] Drs. Schouten & Silver, co-authors of *Almost A Psychopath: Do I (or does Someone I Know) Have a Problem with Manipulation and Lack of Empathy?*, assign a slightly higher percentage to the near-pathic population, indicating that "the prevalence of sub-clinical psychopathy in student populations in the United States and Sweden showed rates as high in the range of 5 to 15 percent."[7] In any case, both estimates are in good agreement with a logical extrapolation of measured pathic percentages across their human-character continuum. So my simplistic (non-clinical) mind can humbly render a conservative estimate that 9 or 10 Pseudopaths could be languishing amongst the 90 ordinary Americans remaining from the original sample pool of 100. Add everything up, and there is good likelihood that some 20% of ordinary 'baseball and apple-pie' Americans will be pathic or borderline pathic. In other words – 1 in 5 ordinary Americans, to varying degrees, are likely to be bad apples. For corporate America, the concern must go beyond the apparent. This nature of disturbed individual instinctively seeks power and dominance, and as Dr. Simon so poignantly warns, large business is their refuge. Caitlan Dickson, an acclaimed reporter and researcher, quotes Dr. Hare's assessment that "you're four times more likely to find a psychopath at the top of the corporate ladder than you are walking around the janitor's office."[8] The fallacious foursome of pathics, it seems, are inexorably drawn to executive positions in corporate America like flies to feces. So I'm going to step out on a limb and "swag" that no less than 1 in 3 executive-level job applicants is a stinker.

That's how bad it is!

For the likes of corporate America, this is an alarming postulate. For the likes of corporate America, earnest consideration should be given to extending pre-employment recognition efforts beyond the clinically pathic (i.e., narcipaths, sociopaths, and psychopaths). Their near-pathic cousins – *that sordid sect of silk-suited Pseudopaths* – should also be identified.

Related Definitions

This may seem like an odd place for definitions, but I'm guessing that pre-familiarity with some of the more uncommon words used throughout this book can only help with reader comprehension and understanding. Particularly where mental-health research or study is involved, things can get a bit dry – and I certainly don't want to add confusion and misinterpretation to already wearisome discussions. So, please oblige me.

The first thing you'll notice is that the definitions are not in alphabetical order. It's not because I'm lazy or disorganized. I am, but it's not because of that. They are listed in their general order of presentation within the text. Because I apply a good deal of business babble and psycho speak, I thought that this might help with flow and continuity. If it doesn't, my apologies. That's probably what I get for thoughting.

I've spared you a re-description of this book's protologism, "Pseudopath." I defined this word at the onset.

Clinical

Descriptive to a level of character-disorder that can be readily classified (i.e., recognized) using diagnostic standards set forth by the Diagnostic and Statistical Manual of Mental Disorders (DSM), a professional reference published by the American Psychiatric Association. Within this book, the word Clinical is applied as a modifier to Pathic, Narcissist, Narcipath, Sociopath, or Psychopath.

Pathic

Webster's 2nd edition New College Dictionary assigns one definition of the word *path* to be "one suffering from a given type of disorder <socio*path*>." For purposes of this book, *pathic* defines a general category of individual whose personality and behavioral traits are narcipathic, sociopathic, psychopathic, or pseudopathic.

Narcissist

An individual afflicted with narcissism. The term "narcissism" stems from the Greek myth of Narcissus, a handsome youth who fell in love with his own reflection in a pool of water – gazing enraptured for so long that he turned into a flower that bears his name, the *narcissus*. A narcissist is overly self-admiring and self-centered. A clinical narcissist is consumed with self-admiration and self-centeredness, often satisfying needs of this sort at the expense of others. The clinical narcissist warrants distinction because all humans harbor some manner and extent of narcissistic traits – typically along the lines of self-esteem, self-appreciation, envy, and entitlement. So common are these traits that the field of psychology subscribes to a concept of healthy narcissism. It is when these (and other) narcissistic traits run amok that the individual's personality can be clinically classified as a disorder. Aberrant narcissistic behavior manifests with constant selfishness, lack of empathy, hypersensitivity to criticism, targeted flattery, boastfulness, shamelessness, arrogance, envy, entitlement, and exploitation. When behaviors of this sort reach a pathological form and level, the individual may be clinically diagnosed with Narcissistic Personality Disorder or NPD. For purposes of this book, NPD is the form and level of the narcipath.

Narcipath

A colloquialism descriptive to an individual with Narcissistic Personality Disorder (NPD). For purposes of this study, a narcipath may be taken to be synonymous with a clinical narcissist. In their book *Of Pathics and Evil: A Philosophy Against Malice*, co-authors Joseph and Sharon Squigna first coin the word "narcipath" as a convenient way to group narcissists, sociopaths, and psychopaths into a single pathic category that speaks to the harm these disorders can cause for others. Because narcissistic behaviors are apparent with both sociopaths and psychopaths, the narcipath could be viewed as a novice clinical pathic. The aberrant behavioral manifestations of a narcipath are identical to that of the clinical narcissist. The executive narcipath harms for the sake of self-exaltation.

Sociopath

An individual possessing a character disorder manifested by a general sense of entitlement, manipulation, occasional deception, situational lying, little or no conscience and empathy, an unwillingness to conform to social norms, living on the edge, a selective ethical compass, and little interest in emotional connections or bonds. Sociopaths and psychopaths bear many behavioral similarities. The sociopath, however, applies them less often and with less intensity than the psychopath. One clear distinction between the sociopath and the psychopath is observable with their demeanor, manner, and social presence. Sociopaths are excitable, frenetic, disorganized and rash, and often lack in impulse control. Psychopaths, on the other hand, are calm, collected, well organized, and charming. For this reason, sociopaths are easier to diagnose (and recognize) than psychopaths. The executive sociopath harms for the sake of manipulation or dominance.

I SEE BAD PEOPLE

Psychopath

An individual possessing a character disorder manifested by extreme self-centeredness and exclusive devotion to self-interest, luring manipulation and exploitation, a predatory need for gratification, opportunistic lying and deception, no conscience, no empathy, no sense of guilt or remorse, no ethical or moral compass, irresponsible impulsiveness, and an inability to connect or bond emotionally. Psychopaths and sociopaths bear many behavioral similarities. The psychopath, however, applies them more often and with greater intensity than the sociopath – in many cases, to the point of being calculating and predatory. The executive psychopath harms for the sake of harm.

Swag

An urban acronym that stands for Scientific Wild-Ass Guess. I'm very experienced with this model of analysis.

Screen

The process of utilizing background checks, reference checks, and other investigative means to establish the qualification and suitability of applicants for a position of employment.

Background Check

    That part of the pre-employment screening process that is conducted with purpose to confirm information provided by an applicant or to expose information omitted by the applicant.

Reference Check

    That part of the pre-employment screening process that is conducted with purpose to objectively evaluate an applicant's past job conduct and performance.

Investigation

    The inquiry, examination, or observation conducted as part of the pre-employment screening process with express purpose to verify, ascertain, or uncover facts.

Pathosis Revealed

    The protologism "Pseudopath" is meant to describe a distinct personality type with pathological roots. In layman's terms, this nature of pathic is a latent narcipath, sociopath, or psychopath. In mental-health terms, this nature of pathic would be categorized as a sub-clinical narcipath, sociopath, or psychopath. In terms of what they are not, the Pseudopath, narcipath, sociopath, and psychopath are not near-psychotic or psychotic. A psychotic suffers from a mental disorder and functions outside of reality. This fearsome foursome of pathics exhibit personality or character disorders and function very much within reality. As

Dr. Hare so cleverly quips, they are *bad* – not *mad*.[9] Drs. Schouten and Silver do a nice job of matching Dr. Hare's word wit with, they are *slick* – not *sick*.[10] I actually assembled a four-word pun that rhymes with "scum sucking bottom feeder," but I won't go there. I guess I won't be joining the ranks of punny authors.

Of the three clinical pathics, the narcipath makes for the least egregious leader. A narcipath is synonymous with a clinical narcissist. This distinction is warranted because all humans harbor some manner and extent of narcissistic traits – typically along the lines of self-esteem, self-appreciation, envy, and entitlement. So common are these traits that the field of psychology subscribes to a concept of healthy narcissism. It is when these (and other) narcissistic traits run amok that the individual's personality can be clinically classified as a disorder. In their co-authored book *Of Pathics and Evil: A Philosophy Against Malice*, Squigna & Squigna first coin the word "narcipath"[11] as a convenient way to group narcissists, sociopaths, and psychopaths into a single pathic category that speaks to the harm these disorders can cause for others. Aberrant narcissistic behavior manifests with constant selfishness, lack of empathy, hypersensitivity to criticism, targeted flattery, boastfulness, shamelessness, arrogance, envy, entitlement, and exploitation. When behaviors of this sort reach a pathological form and level, the individual may be clinically diagnosed with Narcissistic Personality Disorder. This is the form and level of the narcipath. Because narcissistic behaviors are apparent with both sociopaths and psychopaths, the narcipath could be viewed as a novice clinical pathic. In her national bestseller *The Sociopath Next Door*, Dr. Martha Stout states that "Narcissism is, in a metaphorical sense, one half of what sociopathy is."[12]

The sociopath makes for a more egregious leader than the narcipath, but not as egregious a leader as the psychopath. Notwithstanding, the pathological gradients between the sociopath and the psychopath are often blurred. Most schools of thought distinguish the psychopath apart from the sociopath. They can be diagnosed separately per the DSM, the Diagnostic and Statistical Manual of Mental Disorders. Dr. Hare labels the DSM as the diagnostic bible.[13] for both psychologists and psychiatrists. Still, a few schools of thought insist that they are but minor variants of the same disorder. Some attribute subtle differences in their pathological behaviors to the underlying cause of the disorder. In their study of criminal pathics, Drs. Anthony Walsh and Huei-Hsia Wu suggest that psychopaths are a "distinct taxonomical class forged by frequency-dependent natural selection," while sociopaths "are more the products of adverse environmental experiences that affect autonomic nervous system and neurological development."[14] In discussing Drs. Walsh and Wu's research, Dr. Kelly McAleer retorts that "the nature versus nurture debate never seems to have a winner, and for good reason – it is very likely that both our biological components and environmental exposures influence and shape us fairly equally."[15] Some schools of thought would argue that their pathological origins are irrelevant to their behavioral traits – rather, the manner and extent of behavioral presentation warrants their distinction. For example, sociopaths lack empathy, but not to the callous and emotionally-detached extent of the psychopath. Others would add that their distinction can be observed on the basis of organization. Sociopaths are seen as disorganized and rash, lacking in impulse control. Whatever the arguments and contentions, all are in agreement that this nature of character disorder is a very real source of harm to others. Notwithstanding, the sociopath should be recognized to be a unique category of clinical disorder. Aberrant sociopathic behavior manifests with a general sense of entitlement, manipulation, occasional deception, situational lying, little or no conscience and empathy, an unwillingness to conform to social norms, living on the edge, a selective ethical compass, and little interest in emotional connections or bonds.

The psychopath makes for the most egregious leader amongst the pathics. The least argued distinction between the sociopath and psychopath resides with their ease (or difficulty) of recognition. Because aberrant sociopathic behavior is likely to be more open (i.e., spontaneous or unplanned) and disorganized (i.e., erratic), sociopaths are easier to recognize in society. Psychopaths, on the other hand, tend to be obsessively organized – never lacking for guile, clandestine treachery, and patient planning. They are extremely difficult to recognize in society. It is this cloak of normalness that assigns the psychopath its devious, if not sinister, aura. Aberrant psychopathic behavior manifests with extreme self-centeredness and exclusive devotion to self-interest, luring manipulation and exploitation, a predatory need for gratification, opportunistic lying and deception, no conscience, no empathy, no sense of guilt or remorse, no ethical or moral compass, irresponsible impulsiveness, and an inability to connect or bond emotionally. From a distance, one might observe that the psychopath exhibits many of the same traits as the sociopath. But upon closer examination, it would become all too apparent that the psychopath applies them more often and with greater intensity – in many cases, to the point of being calculating and predatory. This doesn't mean that all psychopaths are criminals or have criminal intent. However, Dr. Hares' studies have noted that psychopaths make up a greater portion of the American prison system than they do of the American population as a whole.

A curious variant of clinical pathic is that of the bully. In their book *The Bully at Work: What You Can Do to Stop the Hurt and Reclaim Your Dignity on the Job*, Drs. Gary Namie and Ruth Namie describe leaders of this ilk as consummate workplace politicians that focus their controlling and belittling ways at subordinates especially vulnerable to manipulation, criticism, threats, shame, humiliation, and exclusion. The bully boss' classification in mental health terms is somewhat blurred, overlapping many of the aberrant behavioral facets common to both anti-social and narcissistic personalities – but fitting in neither disorder cleanly. Given Drs. Namie & Namie's postulate that the bully boss' motivations are derived from "inadequacy and self-loathing,"[16] a layman might opine that the bully boss' character favors the anti-social side of the nut house than it does the narcissistic side. For this reason, I have excluded the bully boss category of pathic leader from further discussion in this book. It is important, nevertheless, to recognize that the bully boss is capable of bringing significant harm to both personnel and enterprise alike – just like their second-cousin pathics. In capitalistic markets (like coporate America) where workplace productivity and business profitability is pursued with venerable importance, bully leaders can easily be rationalized as an acceptable evil, given the drive and competitiveness typical to their character.

At risk of venturing into research space outside my scholastic zone of comfort, review of the pathic character in psycho-social relation to the DSM is warranted. Why? Because a clinical perspective of pathic behaviors is prerequisite to the effective application of a methodology for recognizing Pseudopaths within a pre-employment screening process. And, if you recall, this is the second purpose of this book.

The revised fourth edition of the DSM registers precautionary diagnostic advice at its onset, professing that although its categorized behaviors are, in fact, disorders, "there has been little agreement on which disorders should be included."[17] In this edition of the DSM (the fifth edition of the DSM was published during the course of writing this book), Severity of Course Specifiers are provided for each disorder – classified as mild, moderate, severe, in partial remission, in full remission, and prior history. The DSM cautions that these severity specifiers should be applied "only when the full criteria for the disorder are currently met."[18] The Pseudopath's innate ability to fly under corporate America's recognition-radar brings additional importance to some minimum level of understanding about the specific character traits typical to clinical pathics, as well as, to the psychopathology behind these traits. As it is, real capability to spot Pseudopaths amidst the blinding glare of leadership job candidates – and undoubtedly, under the stinging glare of incumbent leaders bent on protecting their own – will warrant every bit of clinical understanding that can be acquired, every bit of related science that can be applied, and every bit of luck that can be had. The clinical part, at least, can be rooted in DSM concepts, and, structured around the mental and behavioral indicators that must be present (i.e., inclusion criteria) and/or absent (i.e., exclusion criteria) for a DSM diagnosis to be made. The DSM defines a Personality Disorder as "An enduring pattern of inner experience and behavior that deviates markedly from the expectations of the individual's culture, is pervasive and inflexible, has an onset in adolescence or early adulthood, is stable over time, and leads to distress or impairment."[19]

Amongst the plethora of clinically-diagnosable personality disorders formalized by the DSM, three classifications stand out as diagnostic contributors to a pseudopathic screening model; Narcissistic Personality Disorder (NPD), Antisocial Personality Disorder (APD), and Borderline Personality Disorder (BPD). The NPD harbors patterns of grandiosity, seeks admiration, and lacks empathy. The APD harbors patterns of disregard for, and violation of, the rights of others. The BPD harbors patterns of instability in interpersonal relationships, self-image, and affects, and, is markedly impulsive. A most interesting observation manifests from the DSM in that neither Sociopaths nor Psychopaths are distinctly classified as a Personality Disorder. Sound reason, however, can be used to group both within the DSM's classification of 'PD Not Otherwise Specified,' defined as a "presence of features of more than one specific PD that do not meet the full criteria for any one PD ('mixed personality') but that together cause clinically significant distress or impairment in one or more important areas of functioning (e.g., social or occupational)."[20]

As revered as the DSM is amongst mental health professionals as a diagnostic measuring stick for individuals with personality disorders (like the narcipath, sociopath, and psychopath), its strict categorical approach leaves many diagnostic gaps where their sub-clinical cousin (the Pseudopath) is concerned. The pioneering ideology of psychopathologist Dr. Theodore Millon makes an excellent start at filling these gaps.

Dr. Millon has spent his entire professional career trying to make better sense and better use of the DSM. In his book *Personality Disorders in Modern Life*, Dr. Millon chides that real persons suffering personality disorders rarely fall into the pure type of diagnostic category that the DSM ascribes to – rather, "Many different combinations of diagnostic criteria are possible, a fact that recognizes that no two people are exactly alike, even when both share the same personality disorder diagnosis."[21] In his earlier book *The Millon Inventories*, Dr. Millon further admonishes the DSM as a barrier that stands in the way of personalized assessment when he states, "Over 25 years later, however, the DSM has not yet officially endorsed an underlying set of principles that would interrelate and differentiate the categories in terms of their deeper principles. Instead, progress proceeds mainly through committee consensus, cloaked by the illusion of empirical research."[22]

Thankfully, Millon provides resolution with his criticism, offering a comprehensive suite of psychological and personality profiling tests (i.e., The Millon Inventories) designed to overcome the arguable shortfalls of DSM-based profiling tests. Millon's belief is that real persons suffering mental disorders rarely fall into the pure type of diagnostic category that the DSM ascribes to. Millon's diagnostic ideologies (and tests) ascribe to a spectrum-based view of disorders, asserting that "Normality and pathology reside on a continuum" to the extent that "One slowly fades into the other."[23] And Millon is no longer short of company in this belief. In her article *How To Spot a Sociopath (Hint: It Could Be You)*, acclaimed reporter and researcher Kaitlin Dickson draws conclusion from M.E. Thomas' book *Confessions of a Sociopath* that pathic behavior is "not simply a disorder of serial killers but one that exists on a spectrum, plaguing to varying degrees a large portion of successful, apparently well-adjusted people."[24] Dickson further quotes Stephanie Muline-Sweatt, a psychology professor at Oklahoma State University and researcher on non-criminal (i.e., successful) psychopaths, cautioning that "If someone is on the extreme end of the spectrum, that's bad, we want to limit their damage to society."[25] A most surprising convert can be found with the APA, whose recently published 5th edition of the DSM (that, interestingly enough, replaces the once-immutable DSM-IV) appears to be accepting of continuum-based ideology.[26]

Continuums aside, if one focuses on the grossly twisted landscape that the DSM inherently paints, the non-clinician (like me) hoping to smoke out occupational Pseudopaths can't help but view it with a jaundiced eye. The clinician, in retort, could bring to mention the well documented prevalence of mental and personality disorders in the United States. As reported by the National Institute of Mental Health, 26.2% of Americans age 18 and older (i.e., 1 in 4 adults) suffer from a diagnosable mental disorder in a given year. This translates to over 57 million people. Another 6% of Americans (i.e., 1 in 17) suffer from a serious mental illness. Next, add the personality disorders across

America – provided by NIMH in two categories. NIMH first runs statistics for personality disorders represented by "an enduring pattern of inner experience and behavior that deviates markedly from the expectations of the culture of the individual who exhibits it."[27] Under this category, 9.1% of Americans age 18 and older have a diagnosable personality disorder. NIMH also runs statistics for borderline personality disorders represented by "a pervasive pattern of instability of interpersonal relationships, self-image and affects, as well as marked impulsivity, beginning by early adulthood and present in a variety of contexts."[28] Under this second category, 1.6% of Americans age 18 and older have borderline personality disorder. Don't add-up all of these statistical variables. Their sum is alarming. Throw in the pseudopathic variable, and the sum becomes distressing. For the likes of corporate America, it's nuts.

The Classic Pathic

Scholarly studies around the three clinical pathics – narcipaths, sociopaths, and psychopaths – apply numerous schools of thought that zigzag across the boundaries of sociology, psychology, psychiatry, and even spirituality (i.e., religion). The most accepted definitions and distinctions between the pathological traits characterized by these pathics can be found amongst the 400 (or so) pathological disorders covered by the DSM. For the pathic three of the clinical sort, a few academic and mental-health schools of thought openly modify their assigned traits, while others would challenge them outright. Table 1 provides a summary, albeit impartial, view of aberrant traits typical to the narcipath, sociopath, and psychopath. Remember, the Pseudopath is not normal like you. Even good people (like us) occasionally exercise poor judgment, make bad choices, and suffer a lapse in conscience. After all, we are imperfect and we err. So, the innocent missteps in our daily lives don't a Pseudopath make. The Pseudopath will knowingly transgress into behaviors that cross acceptable boundaries for human error if circumstance allows. Pseudopaths are of an inherent character that will surreptitiously demonstrate some (if not all) of the following traits if and when they are afforded a position of authority or dominance.

Table 1: Typical Traits for the Clinically Pathic Leader

the **Narcipath**[29]	*the* **Sociopath**[30]	*the* **Psychopath**[31]
Harms for the sake of self-exaltation	Harms for the sake of manipulation and dominance	Harms for the sake of harm
Is Inwardly		
Selfish	Self-centered	Devoted to self-interest
Envious	Spiteful	Absent of conscience
Grandiose	Remorseless	Absent of empathy
Entitled	Hateful of criticism	Predatory
Sensitive to criticism	Empathetically selective	Vengeful
Empathetically shallow	Lacking in conscience	Calculating
Emotionally shallow	Emotionally disinterested	Guiltless
	Ethically shallow	Emotionally devoid
		Ethically devoid
Is Outwardly		
Boastful	Disorganized	Glib
Lofty	Living on the edge	Extremely organized
Obsessive	Arrogant	Shameless
	Shameless	Callous
Impulsively		
Exaggerates	Distorts the truth	Lies
Flatters	Blames others	Manipulates others
Exploits others	Manipulates others	Deceives others
Seeks attention		
Impresses us as being		
Intelligent	Intelligent	Intelligent
Well-spoken	Well-spoken	Articulate
Clever	Creative	Calm
Creative	Charismatic	Clever
Energetic	Energetic	Charming
Tenacious	Headstrong	Decisive
Often		
Strays outside of relationships	Has many sexual dalliances in their lifetime	Has many sexual exploitations in their lifetime

Even as a neophyte trying to 'appreciate' the whole psycho-social picture that this table paints, I recognize a most interesting facet of shared behaviors across the three clinically-pathic categories. Narcipathic traits and tendencies, it appears, makes up most of what the classic sociopath and psychopath are. I will further venture that sociopaths and psychopaths are, for all practical purposes, both narcipaths with a twist. The sociopath appears to be a narcipath with a wrenching twist of eccentricity and spontaneity. The psychopath appears to be a narcipath with a wrenching twist of glibness and secrecy. Given these perceptions, the DSM's pathic focus on clinical narcipathy (i.e., Narcissistic Personality Disorder) should become less of a mystery to the likes of the non-psychologist – like me. And then, given this structured understanding about pathic behavior, the concept of profiling Pseudopaths during the pre-employment screening process should also be less daunting to psychologists and non-psychologists alike. Even to me.

Chapter 2. What Do We Know?

I'm here to tell you, very little. Given the nascence of the pseudopathic concept, there is a dearth of literature about sub-clinical pathics in positions of leadership and the harm they are capable of exacting. But I will tell you this – from what I've researched, studied, observed, and experienced – there is a high incidence of Pseudopaths (i.e., near-pathics or sub-clinical narcipaths, sociopaths, and psychopaths) in corporate America's executive job-seeking marketplace. So, logic would then suggest that their existence (if not proliferation) within corporate America would render many sad and incredulous stories of the mayhem, damage and destruction that typically follows pathic leadership. And we do indeed observe these stories way too often. The news is a constant reminder of the pain and suffering resulting from life savings lost, fail-safe investments stolen, indestructible markets and industries collapsing, and infallible banks failing. And behind many of these stories, the prison parade of calm and charming executives personally responsible for these atrocities are even fresher yet in our minds. A lot of these striped jumpsuiters are not criminal psychopaths in the clinical sense. They are Pseudopaths.

Current Perspective

Not many folks have studied the Pseudopath. Although the existence of the Pseudopath has perplexed me all of my working years, I only just recently ventured into the Pseudopath's chilling world. I do have some interesting (if not surprising) findings, and I'll share them with you in Chapter 3. Drs. Schouten and Silver of *Almost a Psychopath* fame have certainly done some related study, but not with the particular occupational focus that I need. And I've already dropped some names of notable scholars whom have kinda-sorta studied the pseudopathic sort. But not really. So it seems that the medical, scientific, and scholastic communities have only dipped their toes in these murky waters. None have jumped in.

The Harvard Medical School, in its subjective effort to study numerous variants of the "almost effect," has conducted some research around the general existence of a sub-clinical level of pathics. Drs. Ronald Schouten and James Silver, with their book *Almost a Psychopath*, brings this particular research subject to the masses. For this reason, I personally view Drs. Schouten and Silver to be the first mental-health pioneers of pseudopathic study. This is not to detract from the vast amount of study provided by renowned criminal psychologist Dr. Robert Hare, largely considered to be the most influential modern-day researcher in the field of psychopathy. Dr. Hare's scientific and clinical work with occupational psychopaths, particularly in the area of 'successful' psychopaths, are without equal. But they are predominant to clinically-recognizable psychopaths. I've recently noticed research interest around mild (i.e., sub-clinical) levels of what is being called "dark personality traits." This is promising in the grand scheme of related research, but marginally useful towards the concerted development of real-world solutions that keep Pseudopaths out of a business' or organization's leadership ranks altogether.

But if you group the Pseudopath into the broad collective of "bad leaders" and "bad leadership," then a boat-load of study has been conducted. Given the existence of bad leaders for many centuries past, there is a cornucopia of information around leaders that impart harm to an organization and its human assets. With effort to keep things in context with the Pseudopath, here are some of the more relevant postulates and theories. I start with general discussions around the bad leader and then drive towards more finite discussions around the pseudopathic leader.

Bad Leadership

At risk of sounding flippant, bad leadership is the behavioral opposite of what good leadership should be. And to move beyond the flippant nature of this response, let's first distinguish leaders from managers. The leadership ranks of corporate America assign titles like manager, director, and vice president – and many variations thereof. They all manage people and processes, so I'll call them managers for the sake of simplicity. In corporate America, managers have subordinates. So managers are neither good nor bad, because the word "manager" is merely descriptive to a position with authority. Leaders, however, are defined by their ability to solicit followers. Good leaders have followers. Bad leaders are unable to gain followers. Bad leaders just end up with subordinates, hence they are (by default) just managers. So, in a most curious way, there are only good leaders.

I know what you're thinking. So then, Adolph Hitler must have been a great leader? By my summary definition, he certainly was. A lunatic, but a great leader in the strict sense of the word. How he went about garnering followers defined his leadership style and formed his legacy – certainly not the type of leader I would want to be remembered as. But this is all semantic minutia. Leadership concepts and styles are not the topic of this book. I want to focus on sub-clinical pathics that occupy senior-level management positions in corporate America. And because we would like to prevent their occupation of those positions, I will include sub-clinical pathics that apply for senior-level management positions in corporate America. And yes, I'm going to call the Pseudopath a "bad" leader. I take this liberty because it's easier to use than "manager lacking in leadership abilities or skills."

Industrial-age theories surrounding the incidence of bad leadership in business environments tend to view things from the bottom-up. Accordingly, early solutions focused on the plebian ranks of leadership. An enduring example of such a theory is the Peter Principle, a label coined from Dr. Laurence Peter's and Raymond Hull's 1968 book titled *The Peter Principle: Why Things Always Go Wrong*. Their postulate identified a phenomenon where workers are sequentially promoted to a level of incompetence – eventually resulting in organizations saturated with incompetent leaders, which then, results in gross inefficiencies and poor performance. Over the years, this general postulate reached a status of reverence in capitalistic business environments. Well, how times have changed! Today, we recognize that some of the most destructive forces evolve from the top-down. If you watch or read the news, you know what I'm talking about. Business failures attributable to bad leadership abound. A questioning (or argumentative) mind might wonder why corporate America risks so much by affording a select few so much power and control? After all, aren't corporate executives somewhat ceremonial or iconic in nature – more of an image than a functional entity? This question has probably been pondered (and answered) since humankind begin forming groups for the pure sake of survival. Hogan & Kaiser offer an exceptional answer to this question, asserting three major points; (1) Leadership is a vastly consequential phenomenon, (2) Leadership promotes effective team and group performance, and (3) Personality predicts leadership.[32] They emphasize that "who we are is how we lead – and this information can be used to select future leaders or improve the performance of current incumbents."[33] Hogan & Kaiser further adopt a view that abstract social forces are less explanative of good leaders than are concrete personality traits. They offer our theoretical origins as hunter-gatherers as a case in point, suggesting that "the head man is modest, self-effacing, competent, and committed to the collective good. And if he is not, he gets removed, sometimes quite violently."[34] Although their principal message is that the most notable determinants to good leadership are the individual elements that deal with the wise selection of key members of the organization – additional wisdom can be derived from this particular passage. Errors in selection should be dealt with quickly and decisively! I recall stumbling on an HR Focus (magazine) article *Poor Managers Hurt Productivity, Morale, and Worker Engagement* with this very same message. In the article, the importance of remediation was stressed when errors in leadership selection were made. Where *toxic* leaders were involved, the article urged immediate and decisive action to remove the bad manager.

One such toxic leader of modern times is Al Dunlap, who boastfully 'rescued' the faltering Scott Paper company during the mid-1990s. Dunlap's self-glorifying nature is readily observed in his controversial book *Mean Business: How I Save Bad Companies and Make Good Companies Great*. I was amused that Dunlap actually revels in his self-professed prowess – proclaiming that "I took note of laziness, good management and bad, and particularly, an insidious form of ivory tower disease that keeps managers aloof from the gritty world of manufacturing, marketing, and selling products and services. As if anything else in the business mattered."[35] The delusional irony of Dunlap's logic is exemplified in the last sentence of his text, where he unknowingly professes that the people behind the business don't really matter. This is a classic belief for a pathic leader.

The Cost of Bad Leadership

In corporate America of recent lore, "Chainsaw" Al Dunlap is not alone in his hurtful and destructive ways. The exponential growth experienced in the technology and scientific sectors in the last decade have proven to be a playground for manipulating individuals obsessed with some imaginary entitlement to self-pleasure and immense wealth. This opportunistic environment is still in play today – validated by the seemingly endless stream of revelations around incredulous executive-level salaries and compensation packages, pandemic implosions amongst industries long viewed as indestructible, and coy executives claiming ignorance or lack of direct involvement in the face of catastrophic failures. In their book *The Rise of the Rogue Executive: How Good Companies Go Bad and How to Stop the Destruction*, Styles and Smith sum it up with their warning that "executive behavior is the wild card in business performance."[36]

Amongst the many cards that the poorly-shuffled deck of traits may yield when filling an executive position, intellect is corporate America's favored suit. Corporate America demands smart people for high salary positions. The importance of leadership aptitude has probably been discussed and debated since the first leader emerged from the ranks of human existence.

Menkes follows a very structured approach to identifying the attributes, qualities, and acumen most often found in 'star' leaders. Focusing on some of the more recognizable and colorful names amongst successful businesses, Menkes builds strong cases to bolster a fundamental concept that "finding and assembling a critical mass of the very best people should be the first priority of every business."[37] All told, Menkes places cognitive abilities on the order of ten times more important than raw intelligence, emotional stability, and behavioral traits. Corporate hiring-entities should beware, because the cognitive abilities of Pseudopaths are almost always exceptionally high – and traditional interviews and screening methods are hardly sufficient to the task of exposing their latent susceptibilities to stray into pathic space.

And therein lies the problem. Pseudopaths and their pathic cousins (narcipaths, sociopaths, and psychopaths) shine brightly on paper and in person, and hence, seek and easily secure positions of authority and dominance throughout corporate America as well as in all walks of life. Dr. Simon offers that "The various aggressive personalities have certain characteristics in common. They are all excessively prone to seek a position of power and dominance over others."[38] Many are judges, law enforcement personnel, government officials, physicians, clergy, and educators, et al. Even more are politicians, corporate executives, and stock brokers. They are relatives, neighbors, and co-workers. They may be someone very close to you, like your spouse.

A contributing factor to the lure corporate America represents is that conventional screening and vetting practices in business environments are ill-designed to deal with the pseudopathic predator that makes the executive ranks its hunting grounds. Seemingly, all one can do is stand by and watch in fear, astonishment, amusement, or indifference – depending on where one personally fits on the human-character continuum.

Given corporate America's inherent weakness to recognize many of the 'bad' traits that hibernate amongst its executive job candidates, we would expect America's big-business story book to be flush with tales of damaged and failed businesses, victimized employees, defrauded customers, and unrepentant executives. And we only have to visit the daily business news on occasion to realize that – *it is*. From the manipulative misdeeds of Madoff to the sordid scandals of Lay and Skilling (Enron), the transgressions of bad leaders across corporate America bolster the news media irony that bad news makes for good news.

The nature of organizational harm inflicted by bad leaders is both varied and exhaustive. A few entities collapse quickly as a direct and overwhelming result of the executive leader's self-enriching and self-gratifying improprieties. More entities will decline slowly, battling infectious elements bred from within the organization – and fomented by the very executive(s) tasked with their exclusion. If this pathogen of bad leadership is not eradicated, the eventual result is an emaciated and sickly workforce culture. There have been, and will be, winners and losers in this struggle. My experiential observations suggest that winners emerge around systemic treatment that first rids the organization of the infectious agent, and then, ensures that the infectious agent does not return over the course of symptomatic recovery. Further to my observations, an organization's failure to avoid a successive string of bad leaders will exacerbate the workforce ills much like a cancer – from the inside out. Findings from Denison and Mishra's study of executives across 764 organizations lends clarity to this experiential suggestion.[39] Dr. Daniel Denison's work on organizational culture and its effect on bottom-line performance is extensively cited in the field of workplace cultural improvement, particularly around Denison's four-trait model for organizational culture. Two of Denison's four culture traits, Involvement and Adaptability, are excellent predictors of growth. The remaining two traits, Consistency and Mission, are excellent predictors of profitability. Denison graphically presents the four culture traits as a circumplex *culturally* bound from an inner hub that represents the deep-rooted beliefs and assumptions of employees. Denison and Mishra's study revealed that good executives self-associate their behavioral traits with the culture, functional performance, and effectiveness of the organization.[40] So, much like a malignancy that rapidly metastasizes from its tumor, a continuous string of bad executives serves to hasten an organization's cultural downfall by initially weakening the employee's core beliefs and assumptions – in turn – exposing the larger cultural identity of the organization to infectious spread. I present this idiomatic postulate with hopes to stress the value of a leadership screening process designed with the Pseudopath in mind. Replacing bad leadership with bad leadership, invariably, is a recipe for cultural disaster. Entities that expect the same character of leader that caused the problem – to fix the problem – will be sorely disappointed.

I further suggest that the holistic symptoms typical to a workforce-culture ailing from the antics of a string of bad leaders are uniquely recognizable – manifested as wide-spread employee attitudes and behaviors consistent with low morale, misaligned vision, inconsistent values, distrust, and disregard. And from a holistic perspective, no explanation of organizational diagnoses would be complete without the inclusion of Dr. Peter Senge's "Fifth Discipline" concepts and principles.

Within his Fifth Discipline model for systems thinking and learning organizations, Senge stresses the vital role leaders play in the development of guiding ideas that identify purpose, values, and vision for the enterprise. The leader is further challenged with ensuring that these guiding ideas are viewed as credible – serving as a role model whom embodies the values and aspirations the guiding ideas espouse. The antithesis to this precept is that bad leadership champions negativity, apathy, and other workforce-culture maladies across the enterprise. The existence and sustainability of a healthy workforce culture, as such, demands that leaders set the example in practice and principle. Senge emphasizes this notion when he states that effective leaders "embrace the old dictum 'Actions speak louder than words,' knowing that in any organization it applies especially to those who are most visible."[41] You'll find more of Senge's sagacious principles in Chapter 3.

Pathic Leadership

A problematic axiom to bad leadership is that capitalistic business environments inherently attract individuals with outward qualities that are advantageous to making money – traits that are masterfully articulated by the pathic. Dr. Hare (as cited by Deutshman) suggests that, "There are certainly more people in the business world who would score high in the psychopathic dimension than in the general population. You'll find them in any organization where, by the nature of one's position, you have power and control over other people and the opportunity to get something."[42] Dr. Hare is further quoted as saying, "I always said that if I wasn't studying psychopaths in prison, I'd do it at the stock exchange."[43]

Leadership scholars Hogan & Kaiser emphasize that "who we are is how we lead – and this information can be used to select future leaders or improve the performance of current incumbents."[44] This passage highlights the conundrum that

Pseudopaths and clinical pathics present. What you see (or, what you screen and interview) is not necessarily what you get. And so we re-visit that 'dynamic' around the intoxicating lure that America affords pathics. The large forest that is corporate (and government) America demands smart people for high salary positions – and Pseudopaths and clinical pathics alike are typically smarter than your average bear.

The clinical pathics (narcipaths, sociopaths, and psychopaths) are all quite capable and adept at exacting harm on a business and its personnel, particularly if afforded a position of power and dominance. Each harms in a different way and to varying degrees, but it is *harm* nevertheless. The narcipathic leader harms for the sake of self-exaltation.[45] The sociopathic leader harms for the sake of manipulation or dominance.[46] The psychopathic leader harms for the sake of harm.[47] The sub-clinical Pseudopath has a hair trigger for part-time pathic behavior. Regardless of how this nature of leader's gun is loaded, there will be harm!

Within the context of profiling and screening leadership candidates in a corporate environment, a Pseudopath is that class of individual that falls just short of being clinically labeled with one or more personality or character disorders. Webster's 2nd edition New College Dictionary assigns one definition of the word *pseudo* to be "apparently similar." Webster's also assigns one definition of the word *path* to be "one suffering from a given type of disorder <socio*path*>." So combined, *pseudo-path* is meant to describe an executive-level job candidate that – if hired into a position of dominance – will eventually cross the line into narcipathic, sociopathic, or even psychopathic behavior. The Pseudopath will not remain in these aberrant realms, but rather, will cleverly venture in and out. If a psychopath is a wolf in sheep's clothing, then a Pseudopath is an adorable dog that bites without provocation. They are difficult to identify (before it's too late), and accordingly, they must be approached differently. This dog (i.e., pseudopathic leader), if kept in the household (i.e., organization), can cause significant harm to both the family (i.e., employees and customers) and the home (i.e., business).

Nothing gets the attention of corporate America quicker than money – particularly where productivity and profitability are involved. To this end, an inexorable truth for corporate America is that leadership plays a critical role in the financial health and market stability of a business. Isn't that why corporate America lines its leader's pockets with gold? Well, here's an attention getter. As reported in the HR Focus article *Poor Managers Hurt Productivity, Morale, and Worker Engagement*, bad leadership (on average) results in a *50% drop in productivity and a 44% reduction in profitability*. For the likes of corporate America, these are jaw-dropping numbers.

I SEE BAD PEOPLE

PART II

Screening the Pseudopath

At the end of the day, you are what you *do* – NOT what you *say*.

Chapter 3. Are They Worth Screening?

I'm here to tell you, *yes*. Does a share bit in the woods? Are you willing to bet your company stock that they *aren't* worth screening? Because it could very easily come to this! Corporate America's gardens of plenty are teaming with pseudopathic foragers. To the business organization looking at the financial merits of a pseudopathic screen, the meaningful question will not waffle with "if" – it will be resolute with "when."

If the previous chapter's mention of a 50% drop in productivity and a 44% reduction in profitability didn't smack your gob, then you are either a Pseudopath or you work in government. (I'm just kidding about you being a Pseudopath.) Joking aside, you would have to be joking. Right? Because there is no shortage of firm data and compelling information that warns of the significant harm bad leaders can exact on both the business and its personnel. But okay, you're still skeptical. Let's draw a different perspective and look at things from the ground floor up.

A Virulent Pathogen Lurks

In Chapter 2, I touched on Dr. Denison's theories around organizational culture, as well as, on Dr. Senge's "Fifth Discipline" concepts. For Denison's part, I likened the existence of Pseudopaths within an organization to a malignancy that rapidly metastasizes from its tumor – this much in direct reference to Denison's organizational-culture model. Denison's model is pictorially represented as an inner hub of core beliefs and assumptions encircled by four outer traits (Involvement, Adaptability, Consistency, and Mission). Denison found that these particular traits are key predictors of growth and profitability. As it is, the cancer that is the Pseudopath metastasizes from the core, exposing the larger cultural identity of the organization to rapid infectious spread. For Senge's part, I related this diseased organizational culture to low moral, misaligned vision, inconsistent values, distrust, and disregard – collectively symptomatic of an organization unable to engage in generative learning.

So, with Senge at point and Denison in tow, what exactly does a pseudopathically-maligned workforce look and feel like? From my personal experience, it looks and feels very much like the following Fifth Discipline traits – and I'll bet a dollar to a donut (maple bars are my favorite) that many of you can relate to all of these.[48]

- The general feeling across the organization is that no good deed goes unpunished.
- The general feeling across the organization is that leaders do not walk the talk, and, push a "do what I say – not what I do" agenda.
- The organization's workforce will not speak out for fear of retaliation.

- The workforce has little faith in its leadership to guide the organization through lasting and meaningful improvement.
- The organization's workforce feels that they are managed as children, rather than the skilled and educated professionals that they are.
- The organization's workforce feels that disengagement from the "parade" of new leaders and their circus of new initiatives is an acceptable course of action.
- The organization's workforce feels that leadership is oblivious to their cultural plight. When concern was expressed, it is viewed as disingenuous.
- The general perception of the workforce is that the parade of leaders are more intent on fighting for turf, recognition, and personal enrichment than they were for real improvement.
- The general perception of the workforce is that the parade of leaders maintains a false appearance of cohesiveness and only pretends to serve a collective strategy.
- The general perception of the workforce is that the parade of leaders pushes a delusional charter of "learning from experience," then pretends that institutional compromise and oversight (at their direction) is justified by the better good.

- The general perception of the workforce is that the parade of leaders views problem identification to be more important than practical and prompt resolution.
- The general perception of the workforce is that the parade of leaders are ignorant to the premise that most of today's problems are borne from yesterday's solutions.
- The general perception of the workforce is that the parade of leaders seek agendas that disguise over-reaction to events as proactiveness.
- The general perception of the workforce is that the parade of leaders summarily associates isolated events with gross organizational deficiency.
- The general perception of the workforce is that the parade of leaders mistakenly fixates on short-term events, and as a result, suppresses the generative learning process.

Although feelings and perceptions such as these can be widely held by a workforce, they often remain silent truths – unrevealed behind the fears and inefficiencies of the workforce culture. The end result is a cancer that goes undiagnosed and untreated. If you were corporate America, would this be the organizational culture you would want to engender? Methinks not, so me thinks that surely you thinks that a pseudopathic screen is indeed worthwhile.

A Revealing Study

In the event you still harbor reservation, allow me to share a small study I conducted on a large organization that, over a period of ten years and seven successive leadership purge-outs, gradually sunk to the deep abyss from full flagship status within its industry.

It was a rudimentary study involving three simple research questions. For this particular organization, I first wanted to explore the incidence of Pseudopaths and the harm they caused, and then with inferential results in hand, I wanted to determine how capable (or incapable) its leadership-level hiring process was at recognizing Pseudopaths.

The study was very limited in its scope. Most importantly, it was not one of psychology. Although it touched on a psycho-social malady, its true purpose was one of organizational betterment. Without going into too much detail, I applied mixed-method research using explanatory dimensions. Most of the study's design was quantitative but non-experimental. The rest of the study's design was qualitative and phenomenological. I know that this is jibberish to many of you. It is to me too, but I want to include it just in case you're curious. And, because it makes me sound smart. Just don't ask me about sample-size derivation, margin of error, psychometric relevance, statistical accuracy, level of significance, error term, and confidence level. I'm lucky I can even spell these.

I do need to mention a couple things about the study's data collection design, if only because it lends credence to the analysis results. Data collection involved both surveys and interviews. Questionnaire design for the survey and interview elements gave full consideration to the fact that pseudopathic theories and postulates are relatively new. The survey questions also had to be developed with the understanding that the targeted respondents were not qualified to make diagnoses around personality disorders that may (or may not) have afflicted their leadership ranks. Accordingly, I worded the survey questions with specific purpose to establish how respondents *perceived* their leaders, and, how these leaders made them *feel* – the responses of which could then be correlated with behavioral profiles typical of the Pseudopath.

The short of this long story is that the study's analysis results were somewhat alarming – to the extent that an unusually high number of respondents recalled an extensive number of encounters with leaders of pathic character, and, emphatically recalled substantial levels of harm that these leaders exacted on both the organization and on them (personally). Bias? Well, one can't avoid bias in its entirety, and I did apply design measures meant to minimize both sample bias and response bias. If I fell short, I will use the excuse that I am neither a research expert nor a statistician. And anyway, recent statistics show that 93.141592654 percent of statistics are made up.

But let me get back on track. The cautionary treasure that I want to salvage from the study of this sunken ship is that Pseudopaths are prevalent in corporate America and bring real and substantial risk. If you are still in doubt or if statistical analysis and interpretive coding floats your boat, I encourage you to visit Appendix A.

Overcoming Organizational Uncertainty

Okay, so you've (finally) bought into the general idea of a pseudopathic screen, but you're not so sure it needs to be used on each and every leadership position. I agree, it doesn't. And then, your company may be of the sort to forever question the real value of a pseudopathic screen. I absolutely understand. An additional measure of screening doesn't come free – and with pseudopathic notions yet in their infancy – the prudence of an extra screen may always be shrouded in uncertainty. Can the Pseudopath really breeze through the traditional pre-employment screen? What are the odds of spotting a pseudopathic candidate without a screen specifically designed with the Pseudopath in mind? What are the odds of even encountering a Pseudopath in a leadership candidacy pool? These are all valid questions, but they are being driven from an invalid perspective. In this unforgiving capitalistic world, the question should be, can you afford the financial loss the next pseudopathic leader *will* bring? And in the absence of a pseudopathic screen, you *will* hire many.

I SEE BAD PEOPLE

To reduce the organizational uncertainty around the necessity or value of a pseudopathic screen for a specific leadership-level job opening, I offer a simple decision-support tool to assist you in the formulation of an informed decision. It gives consideration to position-specific and job-specific factors, and then, weighs these factors against the organization's relative exposure to pseudopathic harm. The whole process is glommed together in Figure 2, but it's hardly legible in a book this small. You can download a full-size PDF of Figure 2 (gratis) at www.LLSeminars.com. It looks complex, but it's really not rocket science. Here's how it works.

1. First, identify the opportunities for wrongdoing that a particular leadership job affords a Pseudopath. Remember, the Pseudopath is an opportunistic sort of pathic. Here are a few example "opportunities" you can default to. But I encourage you to adjust them according to your needs, and, to add others as you see fit.

    A. The position affords or is assigned significant organizational power and influence
    B. The capitalistic importance of the position lends rationalization to zealous control
    C. The position affords or is assigned militaristic-levels of dominance
    D. The position traditionally demands respect for its power or authority, it is not typically earned
    E. The position oversees operations that are highly regulated or are otherwise subject to significant public and legal purview
    F. The position wields unchallenged spend authority
    G. The position wields unrestricted hiring and firing authority
    H. The position wields unencumbered powers to make and enforce strategic decisions

2. Next, for that specific leadership position, rank the *Likelihood* (L) of the opportunity existing or occurring and the relative *Consequence* (C) of misconduct on a scale of 1 (lowest) to 5 (highest) for each *Opportunity* (O) you've identified in Step 1.

3. Then, multiply the ranking values you assigned to L and C for each O. We'll call these products *Exposure* (E) levels.

4. Finally, there are two decision process paths you can take with the E levels calculated for each O. The choice is yours – both paths are equally purposeful.

Decision Path 1

Agree to a threshold (i.e., acquiescence) value for individual E levels, or, for a summation of E levels. You may want to do this before you assign any L and O values. If you pass a threshold, *apply a pseudopathic screen for that position*.

Decision Path 2

Plot each O by its L and C values in the matrix below. The matrix can be visually used to make a qualitative decision based on densities or dispersions of O plots, graphically positioned by their L and C values. Feel free to adjust the matrix shading relative to your thoughts and opinions around exposure, acceptance, mitigation, or aversion.

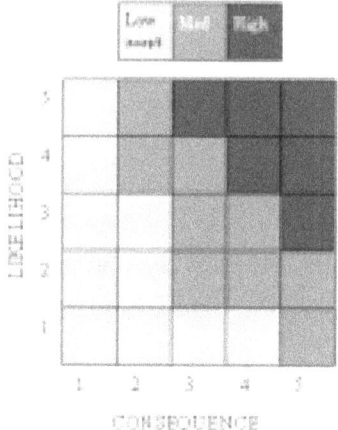

Whatever process you use or whichever decision path you take, the nice thing about using a structured methodology is that it forces you to take all things in consideration in a repeatable and logical manner – the result of which should be a better, informed decision. If a pseudopathic screen is not conducted despite an impelling qualitative or quantitative decision, I highly recommend pursuing measures for avoiding, transferring, or mitigating any O factors of particular note. Remember, you *will* eventually cross paths with a Pseudopath pining for a leadership position – and if hired – you will expose both your workers and the organization to significant harm.

Figure 2: Decision Support Tool for Pseudopathic Screen

(1 of 2, visit www.LLSeminars.com for a full-size PDF)

Figure 2: Decision Support Tool for Pseudopathic Screen
(2 of 2, visit www.LLSeminars.com for a full-size PDF)

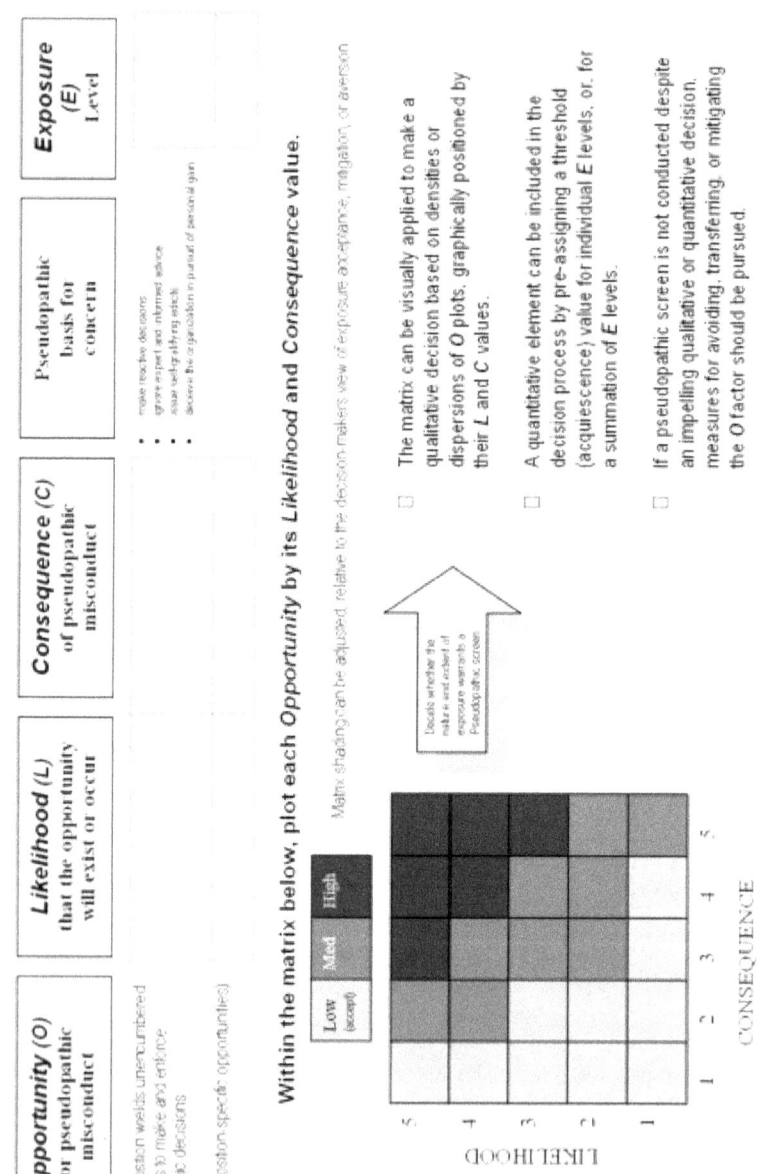

Chapter 4. Are They Even Screenable?

I'm here to tell you, yes. As few as ten years ago – maybe not so much. Today, science affords us this capability. You may be wondering exactly what science I'm talking about – the science around testing, or some other science? I'm actually talking about some other science. But I'll begin this chapter talking about personality-profiling tests, because they represent the most convenient and most economical mechanism for screening Pseudopaths. And they will undoubtedly be the default choice for the likes of corporate America. My immediate challenge is to convince you that they are insufficient to the task of recognizing Pseudopaths.

Pathic Subtlety Testing

Much to any pathic's favor, behavioral and personality profiling tools are rarely applied during pre-employment screening. Where they are not used, the hiring entity doesn't stand a chance of identifying a full-on pathic, much less a sub-clinical one. In their co-authored book *Snakes in Suits: When Psychopaths go to Work*, Drs. Paul Babiak & Robert Hare offer similar warning, advising that "the standard techniques used to screen out under-qualified individuals are well known and little match for the psychopath's lying and manipulative skills".[49] On the few occasions that behavioral or personality profiling tools are applied, the more common ones will be ineffective with the

Pseudopath. In Chapter 1, I mentioned a few of these – like Hare's revised Psychopathy Checklist (PCL-R), the Minnesota Multiphasic Personality Inventory (MMPI) scales, the Myers-Briggs Type Indicator (MBTI), and Geier's DiSC assessment, to name a few. And I'll explain again why these tests won't work – because Pseuodpaths have honed and perfected their skills of deception and manipulation over a lifetime of practice. Simply put, self-report tests like these are no match for the master illusionist and artisan that is the Pseudopath.

And with that hopeless message, I will now back peddle a wee bit. Amongst Dr. Theodore Millon's suite of personality profiling tests (i.e., '"The Millon Inventories"'), there may be one particular test capable of smoking out a Pseudopath or two. I say "may" – because I've never seen it, taken it, or used it. It is called the MIPS (Millon Index of Personality Styles) Revised test, and it is touted as a continuum-based diagnostic tool that can be used to "screen for the possible presence of mental disorders in persons who present as normal."[50]   It is also specifically marketed as an employment pre-offer screening tool.

The MIPS Revised has 180 true/false questions that are appropriate to individuals 18 years and older with reading comprehension at or above the 8th grade level. On average, it takes approximately 30 minutes to complete. The MIPS Revised applies 24 personality scales juxtaposed into 12 pairs. These scales are organized with purpose to profile three key dimensions of normal personalities: Motivating Styles, Thinking

Styles, and Behaving Styles. The interpretive engine for the MIPS Revised test also reports a composite of overall adjustment called the Clinical Index, as well as three Validity Indices (Positive Impression, Negative Impression, and Consistency).

My optimism in the effectiveness of the MIPS Revised test as a pseudopathic screen is driven from two points of Millon's interpretive design. First, he has taken traditional and long-standing thinking scales and "recast these constructs in terms of their influence on one's cognitive style of dealing with the volumnous influx of information required for daily living in the information age."[51] In other words, Millon has modernized this test. Secondly, he has taken traditional and long-standing behavior scales and adjusted them against an analytical model "deeply rooted in biosocial and evolutionary theory."[52] In other words, Millon has socialized this test. Together, modernization and socialization can only make for a diagnostic medium better suited for pseudopathic recognition than your old-school personality profiling test. That's my story and I'm sticking with it.

Even as radiant as I paint Millon's MIPS Revised test in contrast with more customary personality profiling tests, be ye reminded. Millon's MIPS Revised test is still *self-reporting* in its application. And *any* self-reporting test plays perfectly into the strengths of the Pseudopath.

I want to close out this chapter making mention of three pseudopathic traits that you just can't test for. Not because they aren't testable, but because they would be misleading as a screen. These three "ironies" are *charisma, self-esteem*, and *emotional intelligence*.

The first irony, *charisma*, can be identified with effective leadership, particularly in transformational schools of thought. In his discussions around transformational leadership, Northouse goes so far as to tout charisma as a gift.[53] But for the Pseudopath, high charisma – and the elixir of energy that it imbibes – is a disingenuous behavior that comes naturally and is in abundant supply.

The second irony, *self-esteem*, presents a similar conjectural dichotomy. Branden asserts that self-esteem includes "the feeling of being worthy, deserving, entitled to assert our needs and wants, achieve our values, and enjoy the fruits of our efforts."[54] Self-confidence also contributes to self-esteem, and self-confidence is a very desirable leadership trait. But in balance, the Pseudopath lacks in self-responsibility, purpose, and personal integrity. Pseudopathic self-esteem, as such, is a product of different origin from the self-esteem promoted for effective leadership.

The third and last irony, *emotional intelligence*, manifests as yet another desirable leadership trait that shows an ugly side from the pseudopathic perspective. The zen master of Emotional Intelligence (EI), Dr. Daniel Goleman, asserts that an individual's emotional quotient (EQ) is as important, if not more important, than one's intelligence quotient (IQ) towards many of life's successes. He extends the importance of EQ to leadership functions when he states that "emotional intelligence counts more than IQ or expertise for determining who excels at a job – any job – and that for outstanding leadership it counts for almost everything."[55] The discomfort presented by EQ is that pseudopaths, in a disingenuous way, are intuitive masters of emotional recognition and awareness, social interaction, and motivation – all hallmarks of high EQ. More disturbingly, Pseudopaths can artfully compliment IQ with EQ (and vice versa) – a skill they have mastered through practical experience. The deceptive EQ observed from a Pseudopath, however, can be distinguished from genuine EQ when we bring ethics into the equation. The Kouzes & Posner model of exemplary leadership, asserts that leaders must always practice what they preach.[56] Ethics is a critical factor for leadership success. Accordingly, the EQ irony becomes less disconcerting with the realization that the high EQ typical to the Pseudopath is driven by situational ethics.

Further synthesis of these three behavioral ironies would reveal that – between the Pseudopath and the normal applicant (like you) – the character traits of charisma, self-esteem, and EQ are applied in a different manner and with different purpose. They can be applied for moral good or for the right reason, or, they can be applied for moral bad or for the wrong reason. The Pseudopath has a natural penchant to sway to the latter when opportunity permits.

Pathic Subtlety Investigation

As a refresher – the inclusion of a standard personality-profiling test won't do much good with pseudopathic applicants. So don't bother. The inclusion of the MIPS revised test, however, may be better than a poke in the eye with a pseudopathic stick. So I encourage the use of this test as a pre-employment screen on leadership-level applicants. My rationale is – if it just so happens to expose a Pseudopath – the business needn't bother with any more screening or investigation. But I'm going to predict that test-based revelations will be far and few between. Again, your average Pseudopath can game a self-report test with Dr. Hannibal ease. So let's prepare for a 'boots on the ground' investigation-based screen designed specifically for the pseudopathic predator that uses corporate America as its hunting ground.

Thankfully, the investigative challenges of Dick Tracy's gumshoe days are a comical thing of the past. Modern science has seen to that. But designing an effective pseudopathic screen won't be easy, and, it won't come without additional risk and liability to the business. A hiring entity's engagement of detective-like sleuthing can be socially and legally contentious on its own. And then – with historical evidence of improper behaviors and misdeeds in hand – the hiring entity would also be faced with the analytical task of profiling job applicants as near-pathics in a manner sufficient to withstand social and legal challenge. The Bible's Ten Commandments lends explanation to this conundrum.

The final covenant of the Ten Commandments, presented in Exodus 20:17 and Deuteronomy 5:21 of the King James version, is somewhat irrelevant from a perspective of governance. Its literal mandate, "Thou shalt not covet your neighbor's house, thou shalt not covet your neighbor's wife, or ... anything that is your neighbor's," is un-enforceable for the likes of humankind – whose thought-policing abilities have not yet evolved to a level of valid measurement. Of similar challenge to a pseudopathic screening process is that investigative analysis will have to venture into the applicant's mind. This is what the hiring entity must artfully accomplish without the aid of trickery, waterboarding, or Vulcan mind-melds.

Formulating an investigation-based analytical model capable of extracting 'enough' of an executive applicant's deepest thoughts to make a defendable hiring decision is no small challenge. If one thinks about this in practical terms – an attempt to determine what an individual does when they believe nobody is watching, what an individual does when they think their actions are not likely to be found out, and, what an individual's deepest primal and visceral thoughts are – may seem better suited to a serial-murder investigation or a science-fiction novel. But I plead that investigation-based profiling *can* be done for pre-employment screening, and, that it *can* be accomplished within widely-accepted ethical, social and legal boundaries.

Even a test-developer like Millon may agree. In respectful reproach of DSM-based research and analysis models, he stresses a need to "go beyond current conceptual and research boundaries in personology and incorporate the contributions of past theorists, as well as those of our more firmly grounded 'adjacent' sciences. Not only may such steps bear new conceptual fruits, but they also may provide a foundation to guide our own discipline's explorations."[57]

In my final analysis, I strongly suggest that a hiring entity can (and should) capitalize on the epic explosion of accessible information brought about by twenty-first century science, and, can (and should) apply tort-comparable 'more likely than not' decision logic versus criminal-comparable 'preponderance of evidence' decision logic within its pseudopathic investigation model.

For the hiring entities that wisely decide to implement a valid, robust pseudopathic screen, I encourage you to make use of whatever methodology and technology is up to the task of smoking-out pseudopathic job candidates. In the sections that follow, I offer critical concepts and cautionary advice that you may find useful in the development of your investigation-based screen. Because you are heading up an unforgiving mountain, at worst arm yourself with the knowledge and know-how documented from the experiences of seasoned climbers. At best, hire a sherpa.

Investigation Factors

Leadership-level job seekers are invariably requested to provide personal and historical information about themselves. This information is then used by the hiring entity, amongst other factors of consideration, to select the applicant best suited for the job. Preparatory to a phone or in-person interview, collection of candidate information is typically accommodated with an application and a resume. The ensuing hiring-decision process – seemingly straightforward and logical – is fraught with uncertainty and error where the Pseudopath is involved. Leadership-level pseudopathic candidates shine on paper and in person, and, are masters of deception on both fronts. This reality does not favor a corporation that predominantly compares applications, resumes and interview observations to make a hiring decision. If this cautionary yarn seems at all weak in concept, consider the following. Hein Online presents some startling facts around the hiring decisions made by U.S. employers, warning that "44% of job applicants lied about their work histories, 41% lied about their education, and 23% falsified credentials or licenses."[58] This warning bell carries a dreadful tone in relation to the Pseudopath. The application and resume "hiccups" made by us normal, honest liars are poorly crafted, easy to spot, and bring us some measure of guilt. The falsifications and exclusions made by liars of pseudopathic ilk come with natural ease, are articulately designed and crafted, and are well hidden from traditional pre-employment screening practices. Then, to amplify the din of caution, corporate America seems to base a large part of their hiring decision on the applicant's attitude and "fit" with the organization – offering a comfortable theatre and an admiring audience for the finely-honed acting capabilities of the thespian star that is the Pseudopath. If any recollection is to come from this horror film, it should be that corporate America must carefully investigate the backgrounds of their leadership candidates before making a hiring decision.

In pre-employment (i.e., Human Resource) space, the term "background investigation" means slightly different things to even slightly different people. Perhaps, the only consistency is that it is largely inconsistent. Some agreement, nevertheless, may be found if it was defined as a due-diligence process of confirming information and determining past performance. So then, the background investigation serves to verify the truthfulness of what an applicant has presented (e.g., work history, education, etc.), expose inaccuracies in what the applicant has presented (i.e., seek evidence of embellishment, exaggeration, and omissions), and objectively evaluate an applicant's value or worthiness for a particular job function (i.e., seek an understanding of job performance history, financial history, legal history, and substance-abuse history). Some may still argue that these activities deserve individual status as background checks, reference checks, credit checks, criminal checks, and drug checks. Whatever the case, I choose to discuss all in the same breath as a "background investigation." And why? Because this book is not just about pre-employment screening, per se. It is mostly about the wise inclusion of a screening element designed with the seasoned Pseudopath in mind.

The investigative measures that must be undertaken in order to recognize Pseudopaths hidden amongst leadership candidates will not be unlike those of the private eye or police detective. Hankin identifies the dangers brought by this nature of investigation with his appropriately-titled book, *Navigating the Legal Minefields of Private Investigation*. Therein, Hankin begins his discussion by stressing the legal implications surrounding investigations, cautioning that the typical investigator is "still a privately-hired sleuth operating in a hostile world, doing what he has to do to expose thievery, fraud, and other misdeeds for the betterment of his client and society in general – while staying within the law."[59] In this context, "staying within the law" means to preclude the corporate entity's engagement in unlawful investigation practices.

To the investigator of any sort, the most important law governing background checks is the Fair Credit Reporting Act (FCRA) – a multi-fanged Federal law that includes the Consumer Credit Reporting Agencies Act, the Clarification Act, the Fair and Accurate Credit Transactions Act, and a host of other legal provisions. Then there is the Equal Employment

Opportunity Commission (EEOC) law meant to prevent discrimination on the basis of gender and race, and its well-intentioned partners, the Age Discrimination Employment Act (ADEA) and the Americans with Disabilities Act (ADA). Hiding in the shadows of long past, Title VII of the Civil Rights Act of 1964 brings additional screening restrictions to protected classes. Best advised, the investigator need give full attention to all provisions governing consumer reporting agencies, third-party background checks, compliance certification, disclosures, pre-screening consent or authorization, and adverse action. The reality is, these legal provisions are as exhaustive as they are confusing – and failure to comply with the lot can result in both civil and criminal penalties.

Of confounding consideration to pseudopathic investigation will be that laws governing private investigation and privacy differ between States – sometimes extensively. Well-compensated employment opportunities are likely to be pursued by candidates across numerous States. To the pseudopathic investigator, this will pose a unique challenge of broad legal compliance. A concise guide for investigations dealing with this nature of multi-state complexity is offered in Barry Nadell's book *Sleuthing 101: Background Checks and the Law*. Therein, Nadell brings organization to the puzzle pieces represented by the numerous and disparate state laws regarding pre-employment inquiries, investigations, privacy, and civil rights. For the development of a pseudopathic screen, a book of this sort is a must-have design reference. Nadell begins his guide with stern advice that "Employers today must protect themselves and their employees from the harm of hiring the wrong person."[60] The warning behind this advice is easy to see. The wrong selection can easily hurt the business and its employees. A less-visible message behind this warning is that liabilities gestate from the very screening processes meant to protect the organization – and they breed from both within the organization and outside the organization.

From the outside, the executive screening process can foment liabilities from many angles – particularly where a Pseudopath is involved. This nature of dispute and litigation can easily take one of the following forms:

- The unselected candidate may accuse the hiring organization of engaging in illegal background checks.
- The unselected candidate may accuse the hiring organization of discrimination.
- The unselected candidate may challenge the accuracy or applicability of the hiring organization's screening results.
- The unselected candidate may challenge the hiring organization's screening results as inaccurate, erroneous, or misinterpreted.
- The unselected candidate may accuse the hiring organization of privacy rights violations.

- The unselected candidate may accuse the hiring organization of character defamation.

From the inside, additional liabilities may come to bear if the organization makes the unfortunate error of hiring the undesirable executive. This nature of dispute and litigation would likely take one of the following forms:

- Employees may accuse the organization of negligent hiring – claiming that the organization failed to perform an appropriate check of the hired executive's fitness to lead, thus exposing both the organization and its employees to harm.
- Employees may accuse the organization from a different angle of negligent hiring – claiming that the organization knew of the executive's unfitness as a leader, but hired the individual anyway, thus exposing both the organization and its employees to harm.
- The undesirable executive directly brings harm to the organization's employees or to third parties – causing the disparaged or harmed persons or parties to seek compensatory and punitive damages.

From the perspective of a pseudopathic screen, the hiring entity will have to decide which source of liability presents a lesser evil – the potential liabilities brought about by conducting a pseudopathic screen, or the potential liabilities resulting from the ill-advised selection of a pseudopathic leader. Barada brings good argument for the former, warning that "Employers are at far greater risk of being sued for *not* checking than they are if they carefully check both backgrounds and references."[61] Nadell also cautions that litigation around negligent hiring is becoming quite common.[61] In any event, Pseudopathic candidates may be prone to taking matters in their own hands, hoping for the opportunity to satisfy their visceral needs for gratification and enrichment – all at the expense of the business and its employees.

As daunting a picture as the legal factors of background investigation may paint, I'm of the belief that its rigid lines and harsh edges can be artfully softened with brush-stroke ease by capitalizing on the realities of modern-day science – particularly the scientific advances realized through Information Technology.

Information Technology Factors

Relying solely on interviews, resumes, and applications does not favor an intelligent choice in today's job market. Where the Pseudopath may be part of a leadership candidacy pool, limitation of the evaluation and selection process to these anachronistic tools is a bad decision waiting to happen. Conveniently, early twenty-first century technology has provided a custom pseudopathic-detection tool by way of the Internet. So efficient has the Internet become of late with its discovery capabilities that Sprague estimates "roughly half of U.S. employers are using the Internet to vet job applicants."[62] The other half would be so wise to take advantage of this investigative gift – particularly with pre-employment screening processes at the leadership level, where so much is at stake with the hiring decision.

Relative to a pre-employment pseudopathic screen, the Internet offers the following investigative versatilities:

- Employers can conduct some portion (if not all) of an investigation-based pseudopathic "check" in-house with minimal legal exposure.
- American adults, on average, self-publish way too much personal information on the Internet – making it a cornucopia of investigative data.
- There is a vast assortment of online information indicative to the recurrent behaviors and off-duty conduct of individuals – a perfect fit for pseudopathic screening.
- The cost associated with conducting an extensive and exhaustive background investigation on the Internet is minimal in relation to that of a traditional in-house or third-party screen.

The raw advantage that the Internet brings to a pseudopathic investigation can be likened to that of a private eye attempting to gumshoe a case in the small town of Podunk versus metropolitan New York City. Everything is near, public information has already been assembled for open viewing, and traditionally-private information is accessible with gossipy ease. Levmore & Nussbaum articulate this new paradigm when they quip that the

Internet has transformed everyone to inhabitants of a small village – where "No one is a stranger either in the village or on the Internet."[63]   On the other hand, the small village that is the Internet also poses the following investigative liabilities:

- Internet investigations can easily overstep boundaries of discovery that would otherwise be prohibited in traditional pre-employment screens.
- Circumvention of access constraints by exploiting security weaknesses may become a source of legal dispute if information obtained in this fashion is used in a hiring-decision.
- Although much of the personal information on the Internet is self-published, investigative gathering may end-up with some false, inaccurate, and otherwise misleading information.
- States regulate Internet investigations and prosecute cybercrimes in very different ways. States also apply different legal restrictions around a hiring entity's authority to conduct online sleuthing, leaving interstate hiring and screening scenarios in a bit of investigative confusion.

Because the web is but an infant in the evolutionary development of informational sources, cyber laws are relatively primitive and continue to adapt to the technology that drives them. Criminal and tort laws, by comparison, date back to biblical times. Accordingly, the legal ignorance that accompanies wanton Internet browsing (to the merely inquisitive) is easier to accept and ignore. But unlike average drivers who 'innocently' break the law by exceeding the speed limit, are occasionally caught in the act, and may or may not get penalized for doing so – average web sleuthers that 'innocently' break cyber laws don't even know that laws are being broken, and in any event, are not likely ever to be challenged (much less prosecuted) for their crimes. For the online investigator gathering background information with purpose to formulate a hiring decision for corporate America, this ignorance card cannot and must not be played. A warning ticket will not be issued. Odds are, both the driver and vehicle owner will pay a legal price. The wise Internet investigator will recognize, understand, and play fairly within the cyber laws that apply to their online sleuthing activities.

The Counterfeit Access Device and Computer Fraud and Abuse law of 1984 is usually credited as being the first federal statute enacted to deal with computer crimes. Although every state has developed their own set of cyber laws since this time, Curtis notes that the overall rule of cyber law has "experienced difficulty in keeping pace with advances in technology."[64] Major attempts to catch laws up with the computer sciences and wide-area network sciences have seen the enactment of the National Information Infrastructure Protection Act (1996), the Patriot Act (2001), the Homeland Security Act (2002), and the latest amendment to the Computer Fraud and Abuse Act

(CFAA). To the lawful (and cautious) background investigator, the CFAA assigns numerous rules of online conduct that should not be ignored – particularly those rules dealing with unauthorized access. Violation of these rules can be prosecuted as criminal offenses. If circumventing access restrictions, intentional or not, the hiring entity may also run afoul of the Stored Communications Act (SCA), a federal law with good intentions of protecting Internet information.

One may summarily conclude that the federal and state laws governing use of the Internet are so busy minding malicious attacks and nefarious schemes of criminal intent – that the good-intentioned investigator's occasional venture over the legal speed limit (i.e., those benign incursions, accidental missteps, and the like) – will hardly be noticed, much less prosecuted. In logical balance, there may be some truth to this. The background investigator dealing with Pseudopaths, nevertheless, would be wise to heed the following warning. The disappointed Pseudopath rejected on the basis of a background investigation may not only challenge the legality of the hiring decision in terms of cyber laws – a vengeful Pseudopath could very easily dispute the hiring decision against clever analogies to traditional (i.e., non-cyber) laws. Of particular vulnerability to the twisted workings of the disparaged Pseudopath are those traditional laws meant to protect the privacy of American citizens.

Privacy Factors

To the entity screening for Pseudopaths, online or otherwise, the most important legal precautions to investigation will be around rights of privacy – because invasion of privacy poses the greatest liability in terms of potential dispute and litigation. Determann & Sprague identify "three primary sources of privacy protection in the United States: the Constitution, common law, and statutes."[65] The Constitution does not expressly speak to privacy, rather, privacy is inferred by the Fourth Amendment (from the original Bill of Rights) relative to unreasonable search and seizure. In relation to a background investigation, the Fourth Amendment simply assigns basic rights to individuals seeking employment – much like other fundamental rights guaranteed by the Constitution of the United States. Within the context of a pre-employment screen, the privacy rights assigned by the Fourth Amendment are not likely to be in play across the entire background investigation. The rights to individual privacy assigned by common (i.e., tort) law and legislative statutes, on the other hand, will assuredly be in play over the full course of any background investigation.

As interpreted by the law, privacy (per se) takes many forms. McLean distills the numerous legal meanings of privacy invasion under American law and then presents the results in terms of what constitutes their violation:[66]

1. Physical trespass into a space surrounding a person's body or onto property under his or her control
2. Public disclosure of true but embarrassing facts about an individual that this individual wants concealed
3. Lies or reckless falsehoods that alter a person's public image in ways he or she cannot control
4. Commercial exploitation of an individual
5. Tampering with by government agents in matters related to a person's body.[67]

McLean's first four categorical examples represent privacy violation torts, while the last (i.e., fifth) categorical example represents our constitutional rights to privacy. Slanting consideration to the tort-based privacy violations, the pseudopathic screening entity and background investigator must make every effort to preclude any activity that is (in and of itself), or could be interpreted as, an invasion of individual privacy. Hankin summarizes the nature of these wisely-avoided activities as (1) appropriating one's name or likeness, (2) publicly placing an individual in a false light, (3) publicly disclosing private personal facts, and (4) intruding on an individual's "seclusion, solitude or private affairs."[68] It is this last privacy-invasion tort that the screening entity and background investigator must be particularly cautious of. Often

referred to as the 'intrusion upon seclusion tort,' Hankin advises that it consists of four validating elements:[69]
1. An unauthorized intrusion or prying into the plaintiff's private space (his solitude and seclusion);
2. the intrusion was offensive to a reasonable person;
3. the matter intruded into is private; and
4. the intrusion caused anguish and suffering.

It is important to note that the background investigator (as well as the rest of us innocent non-sleuthing sorts) will never be immune to frivolous lawsuits – but protective measures can be taken to minimize the risk to valid claims. The Golden Rule to conducting a pseudopathy-based background investigation will be – *prior to the investigation* – obtain the applicant's permission and fully disclose its purpose in accordance with state-specific laws and statutes. Then again, not even the Golden Rule will offer absolute protection from the legal dalliances of the disparaged and vindictive applicant. Because the background investigator of relation to this study will be determined on harvesting all available information that can be used to screen-out a Pseudopath – perhaps to the legal extremes of capitalizing on the privacy oversights and security lapses of applicants – it would still be wise to have a good understanding of privacy boundaries prior to the investigation. Pseudopaths will be more willing to challenge hiring decisions than your average executive applicant, so it will be important to recognize just how far the investigation can stray into "privacy invasion" space without real concern for legal recourse. Hankin offers simple rules that create intrusion safety zones. To minimize one's risk to tort claims around 'invasion of privacy,' the wise background investigator will seek unprotected information (i.e., what the subject exposes in or to the public eye), will neither trespass nor scope private places, will not use bad ruses to gain access to information, will not delve into irrelevant matters, and will never make themselves a pest.[70] Although these rules would seem to suspend the background investigator's creative license, one last factor of investigative consideration will work to their favor. Today's society is very accepting of openly disclosed and publicized personal information long held to be private.

Social Factors

Nissenbaum mentions an 1890 documentary about ordinary Americans decrying the need for more comprehensive legal rights to privacy. It goes like this:

> Instantaneous photographs and newspaper enterprise have invaded the sacred precincts of the private and domestic life; and numerous mechanical devices threaten to make good the prediction that 'what is whispered in the closet shall be proclaimed from the house-tops.'[71]

Little did these decent folk know that a century later, something called technology would have re-defined privacy in a social context before to un-imaginable and incomprehensible. Today, what is whispered in the closet can easily become common knowledge on the other side of the globe within seconds of its utterance. And today, society hardly cares. Primary school children across America carry ubiquitous technology in their tiny pockets and purses capable of capturing and globally distributing the whispered words – along with a high-definition color video of those who would boldly utter such private things. Our social norms and morays, it seems, have quickly adapted to large advancements in technology over the last decade, and surprisingly, have radically adopted an apathetic and indifferent attitude about the mass exposure of personal information on public display. Nissenbaum views this as a shameful erosion of privacy that will eventually be society's debt to pay.[72] But it is society's freedom of choice, all the same. And to the screening entity tasked with harvesting tell-tale information on Pseudopaths, society's debt is the background investigator's good fortune.

Amongst the wealth of personal information suddenly made public by technology, the Internet is its largest bank, and social networking is its largest depositor. Levmore & Nussbaum take a jaundiced view of the social worth of custom forums like MySpace, Facebook, and Twitter, noting that "Never before has so much information, traditionally private by nature, been so widely shared."[73] Other public-exposure savings plans of popular use on the Internet include LinkedIn, Flickr, YouTube, and Friendster, to name but a miniscule few. And then, this does not even include non-Internet public exposure tools like smart phones – equipped with cameras (replete with video and audio) forever documenting the antics, dalliances and missteps of the bold, ignorant, detached, and oblivious. Another form of Internet technology that promotes public exposure is that of data mining or data aggregation – online processes that optimize the data collection and analysis power of information technology. Andrews warns that data aggregators utilize sophisticated engines that "scrape" data (i.e., collect an individual's interactions with a website) or conduct 'deep-packet' inspections (i.e., collect all communication packets associated with a target individual), then quickly analyze the data to draw conclusions or create a profile of the individual's online behaviors and interests.[74] Nissenbaum marvels at "the extraordinary surge in power to communicate, disseminate, distribute, disclose, and publish – generally, spread – information"[75] that today's technology brings, but then, retorts that this socio-technical phenomena also brings a significant threat to privacy. Hadnagy muses that the irony behind this dichotomy of social value is that the lion's share of private information posted on social-networking forums is self-publicized. I find that sort of funny (in a ha-ha way), too.

A fair question to ponder is – what exactly is the allure of social networking that would bring normally-private folk (like us) to publicly air their dirty laundry? Andrews offers a reasonable answer, postulating that social networking brings an addictive sense of contribution and importance by harnessing the 'power of many' through a process of shared interests, and, by providing "new ways for people to interact with each other, with strangers, and with government."[76] Whatever psycho-social factors of fascination or dependency may be at play – this intoxicating penchant to 'open our kimonos' for public viewing is truly an investigative gift to the pseudopathic screener. Notwithstanding, pseudopathic data sleuthers that capitalize on this social networking phenomena would be wise to remember that there *are* laws and statutes at work in social networking space. As previously cautioned, electronic communication is regulated by the likes of the Stored Communications Act. Online data access and retrieval is regulated by the likes of the Wire Tap Act and the Computer Fraud & Abuse Act. The Federal Trade Commission (FTC) has unwittingly become the alpha watchdog in social network space. Andrews warns "If the FTC believes an organization is engaged in an 'unfair or deceptive act of practice' or is violating a consumer protection statute, it can issue a complaint setting forth the charges"[77] Pseudopathic data analyzers would also be so wise to remember that there are privacy protection laws and statutes in play. In spaces where an individual's personal information is analyzed and applied toward some manner of decision that affects that individual – such as with an entity conducting a background investigation and screen – some of the more efficacious regulations around privacy protection include the Family Education Rights and Privacy Act of 1974 (FERPA), the Right to Financial Privacy Act of 1978, the Video Privacy Protection Act of 1988, and the Health Insurance Portability and Accountability Act of 1996 (HIPAA). Nissenbaum notes the challenge posed by so many regulations that bob and weave across social networking lanes, lamenting that they "are so disorienting as they reveal the inconstancy of boundaries and fuzziness of definitions."[78]

All the same, these social networking factors – along with the unique investigative, information technology, and privacy factors of previous discussion – *must* be synthesized as part of any effort to formulate a valid investigation-based model capable of smoking-out the Pseudopath.

Designing Your Screen

In my somewhat qualified opinion, where the Pseudopath is at play, the inclusion of a traditional self-report personality profiling test within the standard mix of pre-employment screening elements would be a waste of time and money. The inclusion of a self-report test designed specifically with the Pseudopath in mind would be a good step towards their discovery. A good step, but a tiny one, because the pseudopathic dog devours self-report tests like fresh bacon. It is my firm belief that absolute recognition of pathic subtleties amongst leadership candidates can only be accomplished through investigative research. Remember, leadership-level Pseudopaths have plied their disingenuous and duplicitous trade for many,

many years. Accordingly, the probability of historical evidence indicative to pseudopathic behavior is high.

Corporate America's screening methodologies traditionally review and analyze work experience, education, criminal and substance abuse history, both personal and work-related references, and in some cases, financial history (such as credit status). These customary screening factors are entirely insufficient to the task of identifying Pseudopaths obscured from vision within the murky pool of leadership job candidates. To overcome the Pseudopath's mastery of charm and deception, an additional screen will have to be applied. Plain and simple. And where self-report tests play perfectly to the Pseudopath's strengths, your screen must counter the Pseudopaths' strengths and capitalize on their weaknesses. It shouldn't be that hard, because all of the tools are there in front us.

On the very basis of their classification, Pseudopaths are not yearlings. They've got a few years under their saddle. So there will very likely be a trail to follow. No better judge of character exists than the historical evidence of our actions and behaviors. Because, *at the end of the day, we are what we do, not what we say*!

There are any number of ways to investigate and uncover the past misdeeds and aberrant behavior of a Pseudopath – including some ways that would tread dangerously close to civil statutes and social morays around personal privacy. Accordingly, the practicality around your investigative methods should be balanced against the legalities of use. In particular, tread cautiously down that investigative path where monitoring (observation), search (research), and seizure (collection of abandoned property or discarded data) is applied.

On the page which follows, you'll find a methodology (Table 2) that I pieced together with these considerations in mind. I offer it to you as an example, and I encourage you to customize your own methodology that fits the specific nature and needs of your organization. Like Figure 2, it's hardly legible in a book this small. You can download a full-size PDF of Table 2 (gratis) at www.LLSeminars.com. The most important takeaway from Table 2 is that, in order to spot a Pseudopath as part of a pre-employment check, you will need to apply an additional background check that profiles the candidate against general tendencies for pseudopathic behavior. This pseudopathic screen should involve special elements of investigation meant to root out past pathic behavior from Social (S), Psychological (P), Emotional (E), Character (C), and Life (L) perspectives. Your pseudopathic investigation may involve all, or some, or none of the following means and methods for doing this. You decide what how much or little of an investigation works for you.

- Extensive public records review
- Extensive published info. review
- Extensive review of legal claims, charges, and litigation
- Public activity review
- Extra-curricular activity review
- Secondary school records review
- Military service records review

- Social networking review
- Domain activity review
- Internet router log review
- Abandoned article assessment
- Discarded document assessment
- Historical review of physiological, psychological, and emotional health
- Genealogical review
- Doctrine affiliation review
- Personal affiliation review
- Professional affiliation review
- Intelligence profile testing
- Emotional profile testing
- Behavioral profile testing
- Private or forensic comparative review of workplace, public, and domestic behaviors
- Workplace performance validation
- Ethical standards validation
- Workplace subordinate consultation
- Neighbor consultation
- 3rd-party (servicer or associate) consultation

I know, some of these are pretty odd in the grand scheme of things. Remember, the whole premise of the pseudopathic sorts' inherent weakness is that they have plied their intermittent wrongdoing for a long time – and they can't hide everything, particularly in today's day and age. Again, these are suggestions. You may find some of these just too risky or even outrageous – like dumpster diving. You'll be surprised what one can learn from what another throws away. That crosses the line, you say? Draw your lines, then – but do something for goodness sake. Don't throw your most important asset (i.e., your people) and your business to the mercy of a pseudopathic predator.

Table 2: Example Methodology for Investigation-Based Pseudopathic Screen

(Visit www.LLSeminars.com for a full-size PDF)

Investigation Type	Screening Factors	Means and Methods	Results and Analysis
Traditional Screen — A conventional background check that profiles the candidate against the job function	• Work experience • Education • Criminal history • References • Financial history	• Resume or CV review • Verification of work experience • Verification of education or transcript review • Public records check of criminal activity • Validation of personal references • Validation of work-related references • Credit check	The results from standard screening elements are objectively assessed against the minimum qualification requirements or needs specific to the job. Some elements are subjectively assessed against organizational expectations and desires.
Pseudopathic Screen — An additional background check that profiles the candidate against general tendencies for pseudopathic behavior	• Social profile • Psychological profile • Emotional profile • Character profile • Life profile	• Extensive public records review • Extensive published info review • Extensive review of legal claims, charges, and litigation • Public activity review • Extra-curricular activity review • Secondary school records review • Military service records review • Social networking review • Domain activity review • Internet router log review • Abandoned article assessment • Discarded document assessment • Historical review of physiological, psychological, and emotional health • Genealogical review • Doctrine affiliation review • Personal affiliation review • Professional affiliation review • Intelligence profile testing • Intelligence profile testing • Emotional profile testing • Behavioral profile testing • Private or forensic comparative review of workplace, public, and domestic behaviors • Workplace performance validation • Ethical standards validation • Workplace subordinate consultation • Neighbor consultation • 3rd party service or associated consultation	The investigative mechanisms necessary to pseudopathic screening may seem to be more along the lines of surreptitious sleuthing than they are a formal investigation. And indeed, many of these practices are typical to the private investigator, forensic pathologist, investigative reporter, historian, nosey neighbor, et al. For this ilk of investigation, caution is advised to remain within the boundaries of civil rights and privacy laws. Related caution is advised that these rights and laws vary (sometimes significantly) between states and municipalities. An algorithm can be applied to arithmetically aggregate investigative indicators by relative importance — subjectively pre-conditioned by the hiring entity. The threshold for acceptance or rejection as such can be normalized to the specific needs of the organization. Appendix B offers an example of this sort.

The person or entity charged with recognizing Pseudopaths during the hiring process must initially undertake the precarious task of harvesting data sufficient to a pseudopathic determination. Table 2 offers an investigative methodology practical to this initial challenge. This same person or entity will then have to undertake the daunting task of assimilating, interpreting, and appraising the investigative data with hopes of drawing conclusion sufficient to a screen-in or screen-out decision. This follow-on process will be heavily burdened with subjectivity, fueled by organizational perspectives around Pseudopaths and the risks that they may (or may not) bring to the leadership position at hand. But be not discouraged. I have cobbled together yet another model that partners with the previous methodology to form a complete Pseudopathic screening process. You will find it in Appendix B. This appendix details an algorithmic model sensible to this additional challenge, and, purposeful to a more objective (i.e., less subjective) decision-development process. But remember that it is simply an example. No two organizations will want to approach Pseudopathic data analysis exactly the same. I encourage you to apply my Appendix B model as a template for the design and development of your analysis model.

The general thought that some seemingly-normal individuals are prone to aberrant and nefarious behaviors when presented with opportunities lacking oversight and consequence – is not new. However, formal recognition of the Pseudopath as a distinct category of behavioral pathosis – is. What we do know is that leadership plays an important role in the financial stability and health of a business. The Pseudopath, as such, is perfectly positioned to damage the business. Prudence would suggest that

Pseudopaths be screened during the hiring process. The problem is, conventional hiring practices are ill-designed to deal with the pseudopathic forager that uses the leadership ranks of corporate America as its feeding grounds. Commonly-applied personality and character profiling tests are self-reporting. They are no match for the Pseudopath's skills of deception and manipulation. It just makes good sense to augment a self-report test of this type with investigation-based Pseudopathic analysis. The well-seasoned Pseudopath affords an investigative-friendly history of behavioral misdeeds and character disorder.

The threat Pseudopaths pose to corporate America cannot be overstated. Effective leaders affirm their stated beliefs through their recurrent actions – building admiration, respect, and betterment. Pseudopathic leaders betray their stated beliefs through their eventual actions – creating disregard, distrust, and harm. The damage they bring can cripple an organization. Corporate America would be so smart to screen leaderhip-level job candidates for pseudopathic tendencies. It is simply not enough to know that Pseudopaths exist and are harmful. Any business that wants to survive the unforgiving streets that crisscross corporate America must also apply this knowledge and wisdom with "smarts."

Such is the difference between knowledge, wisdom, and street-smarts. Knowledge is knowing that a tomato is a fruit, not a vegetable. Wisdom is knowing that a tomato should never be used in a fruit salad. Smarts is knowing that tomatoes must be selected with utmost care – because some are rotten beneath their perfect skin.

***

Appendix A: My Study Results

Data collection for this study involved both web-hosted surveys and in-person interviews. These are the results.

Research Question One

The first of three research questions (RQ1) asked, "Are pseudopaths common in the leadership ranks of the organization?" Addressed by the survey, the initial question screened the respondent against a critical condition for validity – that is, previous employment for or with a corporation of 500 or more employees. The collective results for the survey's initial validating question (variable 1) are presented in Table A1. A mix of dichotomous, multiple-response, and rating scale questions followed. The final two questions captured demographic data meaningful to the study.

Table A1

Frequency Counts for Validity Variable 1

Have you ever worked for or with a corporation of 500 or more employees (i.e., a large business)?		
Response Options (Answered Question = 111, Skipped Question = 0)	%	n
Yes	100.0	111
No	0.0	0

Data collection and analysis for RQ1 involved survey variables 2 through 10. A positive response to survey variable 2, "Have you ever experienced or suspected irresponsible, wrongful, unethical, or aberrant behavior on the part of one or more senior leaders in your workplace?," was prerequisite to further progression within the survey. A negative response to survey variable 2 ended the survey. The premise for this end-logic was that a negative response was a valid indicator that the respondent had not experienced a pseudopathic leader in the organization of focus to the study. Accordingly, all remaining questions were rendered inconsequential or non-applicable. Collective results for RQ1 variables 2 through 10 are presented, respectively, in Tables A2 through A10.

Table A2

Frequency Counts for RQ1 Variable 2

Have you ever experienced or suspected irresponsible, wrongful, unethical, or aberrant behavior on the part of one or more senior leaders in your workplace?		
Response Options (Answered Question = 111, Skipped Question = 0)	%	n
Yes	89.2	99
No	10.8	12

Of the 111 variable 2 respondents, 89.2% expressed having experienced a senior leader of pseudopathic ilk. 10.8% of respondents reported otherwise.

Table A3
Frequency Counts for RQ1 Variable 3

From the following list of "gut reactions," SELECT ALL that you can relate to the senior leader(s) identifiable to irresponsible, wrongful, unethical, or aberrant behavior		
Response Options (Answered Question = 99, Skipped Question = 0)	%ₐ	n
I feel deceived. He was sold to the workforce as such an extraordinary leader with star qualities.	71.7	71
I'm baffled. Why would someone so highly paid jeopardize their job?	63.6	63
I feel helpless. I can't speak out because I know there'll be retaliation. It may not be immediate, but it will come.	64.6	64
I feel used. I get this uncomfortable feeling that I'm being manipulated for his self-serving interests.	64.6	64
I feel like I have to be on guard. He hides and distorts the truth so easily.	66.7	66
I feel disoriented. He seems to operate behind smokescreens and mirrors.	55.6	55
I feel un-appreciated. My efforts seem to be credited against his personal status, gain, or reward.	68.7	68
I feel insignificant. He professes care and concern, but his actions suggest indifference and disregard.	70.7	70
I feel duped. I followed his directions with diligence and faith, only to realize that it was only ever meant for his gratification and enrichment.	57.6	57
None of the above.	4.0	4

An assumption assigned to targeted participants was that they possessed no qualification to make a diagnosis around personality disorders that may (or may not) have afflicted the leadership ranks within the organization. The underlying concept is so new that even a mental-health professional may be challenged to make a summary diagnosis for pseudopathy. It is not simple enough to inquire whether a leader identifiable to bad behavior was a Pseudopath – rather, inquiry must be made that exposes how the respondents perceived this individual, and, how this individual made them feel. The survey questions behind variables 3 through 9 were derived with purpose to gather this nature of supporting data. Variable 3 data (Table A3) evidences 40.4% of respondents identifying with all 9 gut reactions, 55.6% of respondents identifying with some of the 9 gut reactions, and 4.0% of respondents unable to identify with any of the 9 gut reactions.

Table A4
Frequency Counts for RQ1 Variable 4

From the following list of "gut perceptions," SELECT ALL that you can relate to the senior leader(s) identifiable to improper, irresponsible, wrongful, or aberrant behavior		
Response Options (Answered Question = 99, Skipped Question = 0)	%	n
He doesn't practice what he preaches	73.7	73
He summarily abuses power and authority	77.8	77
He really doesn't care what anyone thinks	71.7	71
He is above his own policies and rules	73.7	73
His behaviors and actions betray his words	75.8	75
He is more interested in looking good (i.e., image) than he is for the better good	72.7	72
He will sacrifice his subordinates for his advancement, reward, and survival without guilt or regret	77.8	77
He only pretends to have integrity, ethics, and morals	78.8	78
He knows how to twist, exaggerate, and embellish anything to his advantage	72.7	72
He is more interested in fighting for turf and recognition than he is for strategic direction or real improvement	75.8	75
He maintains a false appearance of care and concern	72.7	72
None of the above	0.0	0

Variable 4 data (Table A4) evidences 46.5% of respondents identifying with all 11 gut perceptions, and 53.5% of respondents identifying with some of the 11 gut perceptions.

Table A5
Frequency Counts for RQ1 Variable 5

From the following list of "gut characterizations," SELECT ALL that you can assign to the senior leader(s) identifiable to improper, irresponsible, wrongful, or aberrant behavior

Response Options (Answered Question = 99, Skipped Question = 0)	%	n
He is a skilled liar	69.7	69
He has a broken ethical or moral compass	74.7	74
He has no capacity for concern over the well-being of others	68.7	68
His demands are often impractical, if not bizarre	68.7	68
He is verbally or emotionally abusive	71.7	71
He is distrustful or deceitful	73.7	73
He is an articulate manipulator	76.8	76
He lacks any measure of conscience	64.6	64
He is cold and calculating	57.6	57
He is vindictive	68.7	68
He is shameless	62.6	62
He is remorseless	63.6	63
None of the above	1.0	1

Variable 5 data (Table A5) evidences 45.4% of respondents identifying with all 12 gut characterizations, 55.6% of respondents identifying with some of the 12 gut characterizations, and 1.0% of respondents unable to identify with any of the 12 gut characterizations.

Table A6

Frequency Counts for RQ1 Variable 6

Were any of the senior leaders you associate with improper, irresponsible, wrongful or aberrant behavior forced to vacate their position (i.e., "escorted out") shortly after a misbehavior, or eventually after a series of misbehaviors?

Response Options (Answered Question = 99, Skipped Question = 0)	%	n
Yes	62.6	62
No	37.4	37

The logic behind this supporting variable was that the recurring and nefarious nature of harm suffered at the hands of the Pseudopath sometimes results in sudden and forcible termination "for cause." Variable 6 data (Table A6) evidences 62.6% of respondents identifying with this nature of termination, and 37.4% of respondents unable to identify with this nature of termination. A positive response to survey variable 6 was required to access variable 7. As such, 37 respondents skipped the survey question associated with variable 7.

Table A7

Frequency Counts for RQ1 Variable 7

What is your recollection as to how often this nature of exit occurred amongst the senior leaders that left your previous place of employment?

Response Options (Answered Question = 62, Skipped Question = 37)	%	n
Forced removal rarely occurred	22.6	14
Forced removal occurred occasionally	29.0	18
Forced removal occurred about half the time	12.9	8
Forced removal occurred a lot	12.9	8
Forced removal occurred more often than not	21.0	13
I don't recall or really can't guess	1.6	1

Variable 7 nominally quantified variable 6 data. Its purpose as a data-set for study, however, was less important from a standpoint of numeric value or ordinal position than it was from a standpoint of relational support for the respondents' positive response to variable 6. Variable 7 data (Table A7) evidences additional recollection from 51.6% of the respondents that forcible termination occurred less than half the time and additional recollection from 48.6% of the respondents that forcible termination occurred at least half the time.

Table A8

Frequency Counts for RQ1 Variable 8

Did any of the senior leaders you associate with improper, irresponsible, wrongful, or aberrant behavior suddenly and unceremoniously vacate their position with curious silence?		
Response Options (Answered Question = 99, Skipped Question = 0)	%	n
Yes	75.8	75
No	24.2	24

The logic behind this supporting variable was that senior levels of leadership are often bound to a code of discreet (i.e., dignified) termination – regardless of how aberrant their behavior or heinous their actions might have been. Variable 8 data (Table A8) evidences 75.8% of respondents identifying with this nature of termination, and 24.2% of respondents unable to identify with this nature of termination. A positive response to survey variable 8 was required to access variable 9. As such, 24 respondents skipped the survey question associated with variable 9.

Table A9

Frequency Counts for RQ1 Variable 9

What is your recollection as to how often this nature of exit occurred amongst the senior leader(s) that left your previous place of employment?

Response Options (Answered Question = 75, Skipped Question = 21)	%	n
Discreet departure rarely occurred	12.0	9
Discreet departure occurred occasionally	41.3	31
Discreet departure occurred about half the time	13.3	10
Discreet removal occurred a lot	14.7	11
Discreet removal occurred more often than not	18.7	14
I don't recall or really can't guess	0.0	0

Variable 9 nominally quantified variable 8 data. Much like variable 7, its purpose as a data-set for study is less important from a standpoint of numeric value or ordinal position than it is from a standpoint of relational support for the respondents' positive response to variable 8. Variable 9 data (Table A9) evidences additional recollection from 53.3% of the respondents that discreet termination occurred less than half the time and additional recollection from 46.7% of the respondents that discreet termination occurred at least half the time.

Table A10

Frequency Counts for RQ1 Variable 10

What does your workplace experience suggest how common an individual of this behavioral type (i.e., eventually improper, irresponsible, wrongful, or aberrant) exists amongst the senior leadership ranks?		
Response Options (Answered Question = 99, Skipped Question = 0)	%	n
It is not at all common	5.1	5
They make-up a small portion of the senior leadership ranks	41.4	41
They make-up about half of the senior leadership ranks	31.3	31
They make-up a sizeable portion of the senior leadership ranks	13.1	13
They make-up most of the senior leadership ranks	7.1	7
I don't recall or really can't guess	2.0	2

Variable 10 data (Table A10) is key to RQ1, serving as a corollary focus for analysis and discovery. The survey question behind variable 10 is, in essence, a re-phrase of RQ1. In analytical concert with variables 2 through 9, a statistically valid answer for RQ1 could be formulated. The variable 10 data set evidences that 51.5% of respondents would place pseudopathic prevalence at more than half of the senior leadership ranks. Conversely, 46.5% of respondents would place pseudopathic prevalence at less than half of the senior leadership ranks. When combined with the negative responses from variable 2, a postulate to RQ1 is revealed in that 82.9% of total respondents (92 of 111) felt that pseudopathy was moderately-to-very common amongst the senior leadership ranks of the organization. Only 17.1% of total respondents (19 of 111) felt that pseudopathy was marginally-to-not common amongst the senior leadership ranks of the organization.

Null Hypothesis One

Designed from my synthesis of personal experience and literature review, supporting variables 2-9 were meant to emote feelings from survey participants that are indicative of pseudopathic origins. Key variable 10, on the other hand, asked survey participants to summarily assign an ordinal value to pseudopathic prevalence. Null hypothesis one ($H1_0$) predicted that "each of the supporting variables (2-9) would be inversely related to the key variable (10)." This null hypothesis would suggest, then, that supporting variables 2-9 are poorly associated with key variable 10.

To test $H1_0$, sequential Pearson Product-Moment Correlations were used to measure the strength of linear associations between key variable 10 and each of the supporting variables 2 through 9. The correlation test for variable 2 involved a population (N_1) of 111 subjects, The correlation tests for variables 3-6 and 8 involved a population (N_2) of 99. The correlation test for variable 7 involved a population (N_3) of 62. The correlation test for variable 9 involved a population (N_4) of 75. All tests employed levels of significance no greater than 0.05 for

Type I errors. Table 11 displays the resultant Pearson Product-Moment Correlation coefficients for variables 2 through 9 in linear relation to variable 10.

Table A11

Pearson r Coefficients for Variables 2-9 As They Relate to Variable 10

Supporting Variable[a] (Correlated to Key Variable[b])	Pearson r	Critical Value[c]
2. Has suffered or witnessed a pseudopathic boss	r(109) = 0.68	0.16
3. Number of "gut reactions" experienced	r(97) = 0.28	0.17
4. Number of "gut perceptions" felt	r(97) = 0.26	0.17
5. Number of "gut characterizations" assigned	r(97) = 0.34	0.17
6. Has observed forcible termination of a pseudopathic boss	r(97) = 0.41	0.17
7. Perceived prevalence of forcible termination	r(59) = 0.44	0.23
8. Has observed discreet termination of a pseudopathic boss	r(97) = 0.44	0.17
9. Perceived prevalence of discreet termination	r(73) = 0.34	0.19

[a] 2. $No = 1, Yes = 2$ 3. $None = 1$, or $+1$ for each of 9 selections
4. $None = 1$, or $+1$ for each of 11 selections   5. $None = 1$, or $+1$ for each of 12 selections
6. $No = 1, Yes = 2$ 7. $None = 1, Rare = 2, Few = 3, Equal = 4, Many = 5, Most = 6$
8. $No = 1, Yes = 2$ 9. $None = 1, Rare = 2, Few = 3, Equal = 4, Many = 5, Most = 6$

[b] 10. $None = 1, Rare = 2, Few = 3, Equal = 4, Many = 5, Most = 6$

[c] McMillan & Schumacher (2010), Table D2

All of the Pearson Product-Moment Correlation coefficients for supporting variables 2 through 9, as each relates to key variable 10, exceeded their critical values for a level of significance no greater than 0.05. Given these findings, $H1_0$ was rejected. A positive linear relationship exists between each of the supporting variables (2-9) and the key variable (10).

Research Question Two

The second research question (RQ2) asked, "As previously experienced by the organization, did the harm caused by pseudopathic leaders warrant additional measures to preclude their employment?" Data collection and analysis for RQ2 involved survey variables 11 through 14. Collective results for RQ2 variables 11 through 14 are presented, respectively, in Tables A12 through A15.

Table A12

Frequency Counts for RQ2 Variable 11

In your opinion, what is your level of agreement or disagreement with the removal or departure of the senior leader(s) you associate with improper, irresponsible, wrongful, or aberrant behavior?		
Response Options (Answered Question = 99, Skipped Question = 0)	%	n
In most cases, it was an over-reaction to an incidental misstep or to a forgivable error in judgement	0.0	0
In some cases, their value to the organization may have outweighed the little harm they did	6.1	6
These individuals should not be in a position of leadership but may bring value in non-leadership capacities	28.3	28
These individuals should not be in a position of leadership, and, in any capacity pose risk to the workforce culture and to business health	60.6	60
I really can't formulate a general opinion in this regard	5.1	5

The supporting variables applied to RQ1 were designed against a reasonable assumption that targeted participants possessed no qualification to make a diagnosis around personality disorders that may (or may not) have afflicted the leadership ranks within the organization. The survey questions behind RQ2 variables 11 through 13 were derived against a similar postulate. The inquiries for variables 11 through 13 served to expose the respondents perceptions and feelings, and accordingly, responses were meant to gather supporting data for key variable 14. Variable 11 data (Table A12) evidences 88.9% of respondents in agreement with the removal of pseudopaths from leadership roles, and only 11.2% offering little or no agreement with their removal.

Table A13

Frequency Counts for RQ2 Variable 12

In your opinion, what was the overall extent of harm (to the workforce and to the business) brought about by the senior leader(s) you associate with improper, irresponsible, wrongful or aberrant behavior?		
Response Options (Answered Question = 99, Skipped Question = 0)	%	n
The harm was inconsequential	1.0	1
The harm was minor or recoverable	2.0	2
The harm was significant enough to take remedial action	10.1	10
The harm was substantial and warranted sensible measure to minimize its recurrence	24.2	24
The harm was extreme and warranted any and all measure to prevent its recurrence	57.6	57
I really can't formulate an opinion in this regard	5.1	5

In similar proportion to variable 11, variable 12 data (Table A13) evidences 91.9% of respondents indicating that pseudopaths exact major harm to the workforce and to the business, and only 8.1% of respondents indicating otherwise.

Table A14

Frequency Counts for RQ2 Variable 13

	%	n
In your opinion, did one or more of the senior leaders you associate with improper, irresponsible, wrongful, or aberrant behavior cause or substantially contribute to past organizational or operational problems and failures?		
Response Options (Answered Question = 99, Skipped Question = 0)		
Yes	81.8	81
No	3.0	3
I don't recall any problems and failures that occurred at the organizational or operational level	-	-
I really can't formulate an opinion in this regard	8.1	8

The inquiry behind variable 13 expands on variable 12, adding a systemic variant to the level of harm attributable to pseudopathic leaders. Variable 13 data (Table A14) evidences 81.8% of respondents assigning systemic harm, and 18.2% indicating otherwise.

Data collected from variables 11 through 13 were meant to support variable 14. Variable 14 data (Table A15) is key to RQ2, serving as a corollary focus for analysis and discovery. The survey question behind variable 14 is, in essence, a re-phrase of RQ2. In analytical concert with variables 11 through 13, a statistically valid answer for RQ2 could be formulated.

Table A15

Frequency Counts for RQ2 Variable 14

Based on your observations and experience with senior leaders you associate with improper, irresponsible, wrongful, or aberrant behavior, do you feel that it would be worthwhile for the company to check for this nature of bad boss during the pre-employment screening process?		
Response Options (Answered Question = 99, Skipped Question = 0)	%	n
Absolutely not	0.0	0
Probably not	1.0	1
It's a toss-up	4.0	4
Probably so	17.2	17
Absolutely so	76.8	76
I'm uncertain or don't know	1.0	1

The variable 14 data set evidences that 94.0% of respondents placed measurable importance towards the proposal of screening for pseudopaths during the leadership hiring process. Conversely, only 6.0% of respondents placed little to no importance towards this proposal. When combined with the negative responses from variable 2, these postulates adjust to 83.8% (93 of 111) and 16.2% (18 of 111), accordingly. As a general observation, the vast majority of respondents felt that pre-employment screening for Pseudopaths would be worthwhile to the business.

Null Hypothesis Two

Designed from my synthesis of personal experience and literature review, supporting variables 11-13 were meant to emote thoughts from survey participants about the nature and extent of harm attributable to the bad leaders they had experienced. Key variable 14, on the other hand, asks survey participants to summarily assign an ordinal value that describes the need for pre-employment screening based on the nature and extent of harm a pseudopathic leader can exact. Null hypothesis two ($H2_0$) predicted that "each of the supporting variables (11-13) would be inversely related to the key variable (14)." This null hypothesis would suggest, then, that supporting variables 11-13 were poorly associated with key variable 14.

To test $H2_0$, sequential Pearson Product-Moment Correlations were used to measure the strength of linear associations between key variable 14 and each of the supporting variables 11 through 13. The correlation tests for variables 11-13 involved a population (N) of 99. All tests employed levels of significance no greater than 0.05 for Type I errors. Table A16 displays the resultant Pearson Product-Moment Correlation coefficients for variables 11 through 13 in linear relation to variable 14.

Table A16

Pearson r Coefficients for Variables 11-13 As They Relate to Variable 14

Supporting Variable[a] (Correlated to Key Variable[b])	Pearson r	Critical Value[c]
11. Appropriateness of decision to remove bad leader	r(97) = 0.34	0.17
12. Extent of harm caused by bad leader	r(97) = 0.23	0.17
13. Organizational failures contributable to bad leader	r(97) = 0.39	0.17

[a] 11. *No Opinion* = 1, *Not* = 2, *Maybe* = 3, *Probably* = 4, *Definitely* = 5
12. *No Opinion* = 1, *None* = 2, *Minor* = 3, *Fixable* = 4, *Major* = 5, *Extreme* = 6
13. *No Opinion* = 1, *No* = 2, *Unsure* = 3, *Yes* = 4

[b] 14. *Unsure* = 1, *Absolutely Not* = 2, *Probably Not* = 3, *Even* = 4, *Probably So* = 5, *Absolutely So* = 6

[c] McMillan & Schumacher (2010), Table D2

All of the Pearson Product-Moment Correlation coefficients for supporting variables 11 through 13, as each relates to key variable 14, exceeded their critical values for a level of significance no greater than 0.05. Given these findings, $H2_0$ was rejected. A positive linear relationship existed between each of the supporting variables (11-13) and the key variable (14).

Additional Survey Findings

Survey variables 15 through 17 provide for additional findings meaningful to the study. A determinate response to survey variable 14 was required to access variable 15. As such, one respondent skipped the survey question associated with variable 15.

Table A17

Frequency Counts for Variable 15

Based on your observations and experience with senior leaders you associate with improper, irresponsible, wrongful, or aberrant behavior, do you feel that a self-report behavior profiling test would be good enough to expose a bad boss of this nature – or, should the self-report test be supplemented with some manner of historical investigation that digs for past misbehaviors?

Response Options (Answered Question = 98, Skipped Question = 1)	%	n
The self-report behavior profiling test is good enough on its own	4.1	4
Some manner of historical investigation should be conducted in tandem with the self-report test	90.8	89
I'm uncertain or don't know	5.1	5

Behavioral and personality profiling tests are not commonly found in a company's hiring chest of tools, and when they are, they are usually of a self-reporting nature. For the leadership-level Pseudopath, a self-report profiling test draws nary a notice – because seasoned Pseudopaths have many years of deception and misrepresentation under their belt. The most commonly-applied tests of this ilk include Hare's revised Psychopathy Checklist (PCL-R), the Minnesota Multiphasic Personality Inventory (MMPI) scales, the Myers-Briggs Type Indicator (MBTI), and Geier's DiSC assessment. Even the MIPS (Millon Index of Personality Styles) Revised test, though marketed as a highly unique pre-offer screening tool, is entirely self-reporting. As you know, I strongly recommend that some manner of pseudopathic investigation also be applied.

I SEE BAD PEOPLE

This leadership-level screen would be conducted with purpose to flush-out the occupational misbehaviors and misdeeds of the seasoned Pseudopath. In my opinion, an investigative-based pseudopathic test would be as wise as it would be worthwhile to both employees and business alike. The variable 15 data set (Table A17) suggests that no less than 90.8% of respondents would agree.

Table A18 exhibits survey data for demographic variable 16, evidencing 17.2% more male respondents than female respondents. A gender disparity of any magnitude, in any case, is of no consequence to the veracity of this study. RQ1 and RQ2 data analysis incorporated no supposition to gender, and, demanded no prerequisite mix of males and females.

Table A18
Frequency Counts for Demographic Variable 16

What is your gender?	%	n
Response Options (Answered Question = 99, Skipped Question = 0)		
Male	58.6	58
Female	41.4	41

Table A19 exhibits survey data for demographic variable 17, including one measure of central tendency.

Table A19

Frequency Counts for Demographic Variable 17

What is your age?

Response Options (Answered Question = 99, Skipped Question = 0)	%	n
18 to 24	1.0	1
25 to 34	6.1	6
35 to 44	19.2	19
45 to 54	30.3	30
55 to 64	33.3	33
65 to 74	8.1	8
75 or older	1.0	1

The mode for respondents' age is 55 to 64.

My personal experiences within the organization of focus suggested that the respondent mix of age groups was accurately generalized to the sample population. Age group disparities of any magnitude, in any case, were of no consequence to the veracity of this study. RQ1 and RQ2 data analysis incorporated no supposition to age, and, demanded no prerequisite mix of age groups.

Research Question Three

The third and last research question (RQ3) asked, 'How effective was the organization's pre-employment screening process at recognizing pathic subtleties in leadership candidates?' Data collection for RQ3 was conducted via interviews. Sufficient to a participant population viable to sample validity in phenomenological research, structured interviews were completed with 3 individuals. The interviewees were former Human Resource (HR) professionals for the organization of focus to the study. A set of structured and semi-structured questions were verbalized during each interview session. RQ3 data examination applied interpretive coding and categorization to synthesize the phenomenological elements of research.

Collective results for RQ3 variables 1 through 20 are summarized in Table A20. Because my RQ3 interviews were not anonymous, the interview responses have been both summarized and generalized. Data has been de-identified in a manner that preserves the confidentiality of interview participants.

Interview question 1 served to validate the respondents against this study's qualitative requirement for occupational experience within the organization's Human Resources (HR) group. A positive response to interview question 1, 'Have you ever been employed as a

Human Resources (HR) professional?,' was prerequisite to further progression with the interview. A negative response to interview question 1 would have ended the interview.

Table A20

Summary Data Set for RQ3 Variables 1-20

Interview Questions[a]	Interviewee Responses[b]
1 Do you have occupational experience as an HR professional?	All indicated Yes.
2 How many years of HR experience do you have?	The respondents averaged 12 years of HR experience.
3 How many of these HR years directly involved hiring?	The respondents averaged 4 years of hiring experience.
4 Are you familiar with the hiring process used? If so, how familiar?	The majority indicated Yes. The majority were very familiar with the hiring process.
5 Are there differences between the pre-employment screens and checks applied across applicant levels? If so, to what extent?	The majority indicated No, based on policy. In practice, however, there were major differences. Higher levels were screened less often and with less rigor.
6 Are pre-employment screens always used? If there are exceptions, where and how often?	The majority indicated No, but by policy, they are always supposed to be applied.
7 Are upper-level jobs ever filled by edict? If so, how often?	The majority indicated Yes. The majority indicated that this occurred often.

8   Are background checks conducted on upper-level job candidates? If so, are they always applied? When applied, how rigorous is the check? | The majority indicated that this was a rare occurrence. When applied, it was not rigorous.

9   Are reference checks conducted on upper-level job candidates? If so, are they always applied? When applied, how rigorous is the check? | The majority indicated that this was a rare occurrence. When applied, it was not rigorous.

10 Do pre-employment screens include verification of work history and education? If so, is verification always done? | The majority indicated Yes. Of all the screens, this was the most commonly applied. But it was not always applied.

11 Do pre-employment screens check for criminal or unlawful activity? If so, are these always checked? | The majority indicated Yes, but its application was dependent on the nature of the job.

12 Do pre-employment screens involve work-history verification with personal or professional references? If so, are these checks always done? | The majority indicated Yes, but its application was dependent on the nature of the job. Even then, this was somewhat discretionary.

13 Do pre-employment screens review credit or finances? If so, are these checks always done? | The majority indicated Yes, but its application was dependent on the nature of the job. Even then, this was somewhat discretionary.

14 Are you familiar with personality or behavior profiling tests? If so, how familiar? | The majority indicated Yes. The majority were very familiar with this type of test.

15 Are upper-level job applicants given these profiling tests? If so, are these tests always given? | The majority indicated No.

16 Are pre-employment checks and tests ever outsourced? If so, how often and to what extent? | The majority indicated Yes. The majority indicated that pre-employment checks and tests were outsourced often.

17 What are your thoughts and opinions around the survey findings? | The majority agreed and personally identified with the survey findings.

18 Based on survey findings, do you feel that a Pseudopathic job candidate can make it through the the organization's pre-employment checks un-noticed?	The majority indicated Yes.
19 In your opinion, would a MIPS-based test add value as a pre-employment check? If so, do you think that the organization needs a test like MIPS ?	The majority indicated Yes.
20 Personality and behavior profiling tests, including MIPS, are self-reporting. Do you think that a trait-based historical investigation would add value as a pre-employment check? If so, do you think that the organization needs this nature of pre-employment check?	The majority indicated Yes.

a The interview questions are summarized.

b The interview responses are both summarized and generalized. Data has been de-identified in a manner that preserves the confidentiality of interview participants.

The interview responses provided the qualitative platform for RQ3 data analysis. Interview transcriptions were reviewed in detail and depth, issues were clustered into common themes, and then succinct descriptions of central phenomena were constructed. Table A21 identifies the themes generated from the interview responses, frequency counts relating to each theme, and coding points between the respondents.

Table A21

Themes, Frequency Counts, and Coding Points for RQ3 Interview Responses

Theme	n	Respondent Coding Points[a]		
		1	2	3
Pre-employment screens and checks are neither consistently nor rigorously applied on senior and executive job candidates at the company	3	1	3	3
Personality and behavioral profiling tests are not applied on senior and executive job candidates at the company.	3	3	3	3
Pseudopathic job candidates at the senior and executive levels are not at risk of being discovered by the company as a result of pre-employment screens and checks	3	2	3	3
Trait-based historical investigation of senior and executive level job applicants at the company would be more effective at discovering Pseudopaths than a self-report test would be	3	2	3	3

[a] *Somewhat Sure* = 1, *Sure* = 2, *Very Sure* = 3

In interpretive analysis for RQ3, the accumulation of 36 coding points would be sufficient to a response with absolute (100%) certainty of the respondents' experiences, opinions, or perceptions formative to the assigned themes. Given a coding point total of 32 points for the interview responses, RQ3 can be answered with good (88%) certainty in their collective regard.

Research Question One Findings

RQ1 asked, "Were pseudopaths common in the leadership ranks of the organization?" The quantitative analysis of data assimilated from the study's survey affirmed that Pseudopaths were common in the leadership ranks of the organization of focus to the study. Within the survey, seven RQ1 variables served in a support role for a key RQ1 varaiable. An overwhelming number of key-variable respondents felt that Pseudopaths served in the leadership ranks of the organization, and, that their existence was a common occurrence within the. Data from the seven support variables confirmed that the respondents collectively understood the Pseudopathic concept by way of trait, character, and behavior, and, soundly related this understanding to the recognition of Pseudopaths in leadership roles. Correlation testing of RQ1 survey data validated the generalization of an RQ1 solution to the larger population studied for the organization.

Research Question Two Findings

RQ2 asked, "As previously experienced by the organization, did the harm caused by pseudopathic leaders warrant additional measures to preclude their employment?" The quantitative analysis of data assimilated from the study's survey affirms that the harm caused by pseudopathic leaders (previously experienced within the organization) warranted additional measures to preclude their employment. Within the survey, three RQ2 variables served in a support role for a key RQ2 varaiable. An overwhelming number of key-variable respondents felt that the harm caused by leadership-level Pseudopaths to both personnel and business within the organization demanded preventative measures that would keep the pseudopathic type out of leadership positions. Data from the three support variables confirmed that the respondents collectively understood the nature and extent of harm attributable to pseudopathic leaders, and, soundly related this understanding to the assignment of pseudopathic harm suffered by the organization. Correlation testing of RQ2 survey data validated the generalization of an RQ2 solution to the larger population studied for the organization.

Research Question Three Findings

RQ3 asked, "How effective was the organization's pre-employment screening process at recognizing pathic subtleties in leadership candidates?' The qualitative analysis of data assimilated from the study's interviews affirms that the organization's pre-employment screening process was ineffective at recognizing pathic subtleties in leadership candidates. Interpretive coding of interview responses yielded four thematic observations for RQ3. The first theme evidenced moderate certainty that the organization's pre-employment screens and checks were neither consistently nor rigorously applied on senior and executive job candidates. The second theme evidenced high certainty that personality and behavioral profiling tests were not applied on senior and executive job candidates for the organization. The third theme evidenced high certainty that pseudopathic job candidates at the senior and executive levels were not at risk of being discovered by the organization as a result of pre-employment screens and checks. The fourth and final theme evidenced high certainty that trait-based historical investigation of senior and executive level job applicants would be more effective at discovering Pseudopaths than a self-report test would be for the organization.

Concluding Note

In balance with other "bad leader" studies I had conducted, I found the results from this particular study a bit startling. In current reflection, I'm beginning to wonder whether these results really shouldn't have come as a surprise. The Pseudopathic predator roams freely within corporate America, and the harm they are capable of inflicting on both personnel and business is something us simple folk just can't forgive and forget.

Appendix B: Example Screening Model

Corporate America's pre-employment screens, when applied, typically review work experience, education, criminal and substance abuse history, both personal and work-related references, and in some cases, financial history (such as credit status). These pre-employment screening factors are largely insufficient to the task of identifying leadership-level Pseudopaths. In Chapter 4, I presented an example methodology for conducting a historically-based pseudopathic screen. Whatever methodology you choose to apply, the entity charged with recognizing Pseudopaths lurking amongst candidates being considered for a leadership position must first undertake the precarious task of harvesting data sufficient to a pseudopathic determination. The investigating entity will then have to undertake the daunting task of assimilating, interpreting, and appraising the investigated data with hopes of drawing conclusion sufficient to a screen-in or screen-out decision. This follow-on process will be heavily burdened with subjectivity fueled by organizational perspectives around Pseudopaths and the risks they would bring to the executive position at hand.

That's what I hope to help with here. I am neither a mathematician nor a statistician, but I'm marginally capable of combining logic with the three "Rs" I was learned in grade school (reading, righting, and rithmetic). No matter, the algorithm I'm about to present is an example. I offer it to you as a general source of information and, hopefully, as a starting point for crafting a decision-support algorithm that best fits your needs.

The construct of this proposed algorithm demanded simple and practical thought-processes capable of recognizing the Pseudopath at the low end of the pathic continuum, yet sensitive to the occasional misjudgments, misdeeds, and missteps normal to human life in this unforgiving world. From afar, I think that the results of my algorithmic efforts – cobbled together with rudimentary mathematics, objective variables, and qualitative factors of consideration – are neither elegant nor perfect. The application of its sort within your overall hiring process, however, is likely to be more rewarding than a poke in the eye with a pseudopathic stick.

Much like the psycho-analytical process of uncovering a patient's mental disorder is part science and part art, the analytical mechanics of the proposed algorithm are hardly an exact science. Effort was made, however, to apply probabilistic sense to its computational design and structure. (On a side note, the following presentation is a bit "cluttery" for such a small book. Visit www.LLSeminars.com for a full-size PDF of the algorithm.)

With purpose to minimize the subjective elements of analysis and to normalize investigative data relative to the organization's needs and perceptions, the algorithm's computational engine will apply the following bi-modal weighting logic:

- The pseudopathic profiling element, defined as X, will be comparatively ranked against traditional pre-employment screening factors by relative importance (as determined by the hiring organization).

- The individual pseudopathic screening elements, identified as A through E, will be comparatively ranked against each other by relative importance (as determined by the hiring organization).

Preparatory to the adoption of pseudopathic screening results towards an employment decision, the hiring organization will be asked to assign a weighting factor (x) that represents the importance of the pseudopathic profiling element relative to other pre-employment screening elements customary to the organization.

For sake of example, the customary screening elements will be taken to be:

R   Education and Training
S   Professional Experience and History
T   Credit History
U   Criminal History

The following assumptions are prerequisite to the assignment of a viable weighting factor:

- The hiring organization both desires and undertakes the pseudopathic screen. That is, its importance to the hiring organization relative to other screening elements (R through U) is not zero.

- The pseudopathic screen is not singularly important to the hiring decision. That is, one or more other pre-employment screening factors (R through U) will be of influence to the hiring decision.

Refer to Figure B1. The hiring organization will valuate weighting-factor x as a whole number between 0 and 100 (i.e., from 1 to 99) relative to the pseudopathic screen's comparative importance to screening elements R through U. The hiring organization will also assign values of importance for R through U, their total of which must equal 100. Figure B1 provides a diagrammatic explanation of weighting-factor x, as well as rank examples of assigned weighting values.

Figure B1 Weighting Factor x (with rank examples)

NOT IMPORTANT (x = 0) ←→ SHARED IMPORTANCE (x = 1 to 99) ←→ SINGULARLY IMPORTANT (x = 100)

where x represents the importance of the pseudopathic screen relative to screening elements R through U

Example 1
x = 1
R = 40
S = 49
T = 0
U = 10

Example 2
x = 20
R = 20
S = 20
T = 20
U = 20

Example 3
x = 80
R = 9
S = 9
T = 1
U = 1

where the value of x will be used to counterweight pseudopathic profiling element X

Relating to Table 2, the individual pseudopathic screening elements will be categorically represented as follows:

    A   Social Elements
    B   Psychological Elements
    C   Emotional Elements
    D   Character Elements
    E   Life Elements

Pseudopathic screening elements A through E will be quantified as the number of pseudopathic "hits" (i.e., behavioral and trait-based anomalies) uncovered, discovered, or observed for each element through investigative means. For Table 2, hits assignable to A through E are characterized as follows:

    Quantity A = The number of investigative hits (instances, events, or circumstances) evidential to (a, b, c, i) behaviors or traits in a social environment or of a social nature

    Quantity B = The number of investigative hits (instances, events, or circumstances) evidential to (c, d, e, f, l) behaviors or traits of a psychological nature or mental state of mind

    Quantity C = The number of investigative hits (instances, events, or circumstances) evidential to (c, f, h, k, l) behaviors or traits of an emotional or dispositional nature

Quantity D = The number of investigative hits (instances, events, or circumstances) evidential to (b, d thru l) behaviors or traits indicative to character, personality, or inherent nature

Quantity E = The number of investigative hits (instances, events, or circumstances) evidential to (c, d, e, f, g, h, i) behaviors or traits around life, family, or personal relationships

Where
- (a) = unlawful or otherwise illicit
- (b) = disingenuous, unscrupulous, or similarly improper
- (c) = aberrant or extreme
- (d) = unethical or immoral
- (e) = untruthful, deceptive, duplicitous, or manipulative
- (f) = abusive or similarly harmful
- (g) = accusatory, contentious, or litigious
- (h) = uncaring or insensitive
- (i) = deviant or indiscrete
- (j) = boastful, arrogant, or callous
- (k) = calculating or predatory
- (l) = shameless or remorseless

Using the above characteristics as a cross-reference, the hiring organization will rank each pseudopathic screening element (A though E) by their relative importance to the organization.

1 Not Important
2 Somewhat Important
3 Important
4 Very Important
5 Critically Important

A baseline screen-in (i.e., threshold) value, z, is established with experiential logic and absolutes. There is every reason to accept a postulate that zero investigative hits is absolute to a screen-out decision. Conversely, there is little reason to reject a postulate that a pattern of recurrent hits across a majority of the pseudopathic screening categories is absolute to a screen-in decision. Mimicking diagnostic standards typical to the mental-health examinations recommended by Dr. Zimmerman,[79] one can rationalize that an average of 2 investigative hits within a single category of pseudopathic screen is sufficient to a recurrent pattern, and, that an average of 3 applicable categories is sufficient to a majority of the 5 available categories. The combined rationalization affords a credible postulate that – 2 investigative hits in each of any 3 pseudopathic screening categories of average and equal importance – is sufficient to an average threshold value for a screen-in decision. A related postulate is afforded to the effect that an investigated quantity of hits between zero and five, and/or, an observation of hits in less than 3 pseudopathic screening categories, introduces an uncomfortable margin of uncertainty. This logic baselines a pseudopathic threshold value as follows:

$$\text{The Baseline Threshold Value } (z) = \text{No. of hits absolute to a screen-in} \cdot \text{The avg. weighting factor} \quad (1)$$

$$z = 6 \cdot 3$$

$$z = 18$$

The normalized threshold value, Z, will be derived from the baseline value (z) and applied as a decision point in contrast with the investigated value of pseudopathic profile X. The value of Z will skew positive or negative from the value of z (prescribed as 18) as a function of x (reference Figure B2).

Where Z is negatively skewed by f(x), the resulting threshold value will err to the hiring detriment of the Pseudopath. Where Z is positively skewed by f(x), the resulting threshold value will err to the hiring favor of the

I SEE BAD PEOPLE

Pseudopath. The magnitude and vector (i.e., direction) of influence presented to z by f(x) is established as follows:

$$\text{Determine the ratio of } x \text{ to } (R+S+T+U) \qquad (2)$$

$$\begin{array}{ll} \text{If this ratio is between 3.1 and 99, then } Z = z - 4 = & 14 \\ \text{If this ratio is between 1 and 3.1, then } Z = z - 2 = & 16 \\ \text{If this ratio is 1, then } Z = & 18 \\ \text{If this ratio is between 0.32 and 1, then } Z = z + 2 = & 20 \\ \text{If this ratio is between .01 and 0.32, then } Z = z + 4 = & 22 \end{array}$$

Objective coalescence of the precepts described above yields a pseudopathic screening algorithm of the following form:

$$X = \sum_{i=A}^{E} (H_i)(W_i) \qquad (3)$$

Where H = No. of investigated hits for each of the pseudopathic screening elements A through E

W = Weighting factor assigned to each of the pseudopathic screening elements A through E

X = Numeric value of the pseudopathic profile element

And where:

Analytical confidence is contingent on achieving 2 or more hits in each of at least 3 pseudopathic screening categories A through E. Where this condition is not met, X will be considered invalid to a screen-in decision made with the pseudopathic threshold Z.

	Example 1				Example 2		
	H	W	Prod		H	W	Prod
A	2	5	10	A	1	5	5
B	1	5	5	B	0	5	0
C	0	3	0	C	1	3	3
D	2	1	2	D	5	2	10
E	2	1	2	E	4	1	4
		Sum	19			Sum	22

∴ X is valid to Z   ∴ X is invalid to Z

Where X is invalid to Z, the algorithmic conclusion will be that the job applicant, *more-than-likely*, **WILL MEET** the hiring organization's character expectations for a leader.

Where X is valid to Z, and, where the value of X is less than the value of Z, the algorithmic conclusion will be that the job applicant, *more-than-likely*, **WILL MEET** the hiring organization's character expectations for a leader.

Where X is valid to Z, and, where the value of X equals or exceeds the value of Z, the algorithmic conclusion will be that the job applicant, *more-than-likely*, **WILL NOT MEET** the hiring organization's character expectations for a leader.

End Notes

1. Babiak, P. & Hare R, *SnakesIn Suits: When Psychopaths Go to Work* (2006): 103.
2. Simon, G., *In Sheep's Clothing: Understanding and Dealing with Manipulative People* (2010): 32.
3. Babiak, P. & Hare R, *SnakesIn Suits: When Psychopaths Go to Work* (2006).
4. Stout, M., *The Sociopath Next Door* (2005).
5. Babiak, P. & Hare R, *SnakesIn Suits: When Psychopaths Go to Work* (2006).
6. Babiak, P. & Hare R, *SnakesIn Suits: When Psychopaths Go to Work* (2006): 177.
7. Schouten, R. & Silver, J., *Almost aPpsychopath: Do I (or Does Someone I Know) Have a Problem with Manipulation andLack of Empathy?* (2012): 57.
8. Dickson, C., How to Spot a Sociopath (Hint: It Could Be You). *The Daily Beast* (2013, June): Para. 3.
9. Hare, R., *Without conscience: The Disturbing World of the Psychopaths Among Us* (1993): 5.
10. Schouten, R. & Silver, J., *Almost aPpsychopath: Do I (or Does Someone I Know) Have a Problem with Manipulation andLack of Empathy?* (2012): 201.
11. Squigna, J. & Squigna, S., *Of Pathics and Evil* (2009): 9.
12. Stout, M., *The Sociopath Next Door* (2005): 127.

13. Hare, R., *Without conscience: The Disturbing World of the Psychopaths Among Us* (1993): 24.
14. McAleer, K., Sociopathy vs. Psychopathy. *Psych Central* (2010): Para. 4.
15. McAleer, K., Sociopathy vs. Psychopathy. *Psych Central* (2010): Para. 5.
16. Namie, G. & Namie, R., *The Bully at Work: What You Can Do to Stop the Hurt and Reclaim Your Dignity On the Job* (2010): 14.
17. DSM-IV-TR, American Psychiatric Association. *Diagnostic and Statistical Manual of Mental Disorders: Text Revision* (4th Edition, 2000): xxiv.
18. DSM-IV-TR, American Psychiatric Association. *Diagnostic and Statistical Manual of Mental Disorders: Text Revision* (4th Edition, 2000): 2.
19. DSM-IV-TR, American Psychiatric Association. *Diagnostic and Statistical Manual of Mental Disorders: Text Revision* (4th Edition, 2000): 685.
20. DSM-IV-TR, American Psychiatric Association. *Diagnostic and Statistical Manual of Mental Disorders: Text Revision* (4th Edition, 2000): 729.
21. Millon, T., Grossman, S., Millon, C., Meagher, S. & Ramnath, R., *Personality Disorders In Modern Life* (2nd Edition, 2004): 8.

22. Millon, T., Grossman, S., Millon, C., Meagher, S. & Ramnath, R., *Personality Disorders In Modern Life* (2nd Edition, 2004): 8.
23. Millon, T., Grossman, S., Millon, C., Meagher, S. & Ramnath, R., *Personality Disorders In Modern Life* (2nd Edition, 2004): 12.
24. Dickson, C., How to Spot a Sociopath (Hint: It Could Be You). *The Daily Beast* (2013, June): Para. 2.
25. Stephanie Muline-Sweatt cited by Dickson, C., How to Spot a Sociopath (Hint: It Could Be You). *The Daily Beast* (2013, June): Para. 5.
26. Much of the literary research associated with this work was conducted over a period when the fourth edition of the DSM served as the diagnostic standard for mental health professionals. Prior to its completion, the fifth edition of the DSM was released for occupational use. The quoted references from page xxiv (re. little agreement on disorders) and page 2 (re. Severity of Course Specifiers) of the DSM-IV do not exist in the DSM-5. The quoted reference from page 685 of the DSM-IV can be found on page 645 of the DSM-5. The quoted reference from page 729 (re. Personality Disorder Not Otherwise Specified) of the DSM-IV does not exist in the DSM-5. All referenced works and quotes of Dr. Millon relate to the DSM-IV. The DSM-5 brings significant change to many facets of diagnostic measure

and analysis – including that of continuum concepts and "more informative diagnosis for individuals who are not optimally described as having a specific personality disorder" (p. 816). A new clinical category of disorder, titled the Alternative DSM-5 Model for Personality Disorders, is provided to cover patients that "do not tend to present with patterns of symptoms that correspond with one and only one personality disorder" (p. 761).

27. Mental Disorders in America, *National Institute of Mental Health* (2013), a component of the U.S. Department of Health and Human Services.

28. Mental Disorders in America, *National Institute of Mental Health* (2013), a component of the U.S. Department of Health and Human Services.

29. Squigna, J. & Squigna, S., *Of Pathics and Evil* (2009).

30. Stout, M., *The Sociopath Next Door* (2005).

31. Primary reference: Ronson, J., *The Psychopath Test: A Journey Through the Madness Industry* (2011). Secondary references: Babiak, P. & Hare R, *SnakesIn Suits: When Psychopaths Go to Work* (2006). Hare, R., *Without conscience: The Disturbing World of the Psychopaths Among Us* (1993). Simon, G., *In Sheep's Clothing: Understanding and Dealing with Manipulative People* (2010).

32. Hogan, R., & Kaiser, R., What We Know About Leadership. *Review of General Psychology* (2005).

33. Hogan, R., & Kaiser, R., What We Know About Leadership. *Review of General Psychology* (2005): 170.
34. Hogan, R., & Kaiser, R., What We Know About Leadership. *Review of General Psychology* (2005): 174.
35. Dunlap, A., *Mean Business: How I Save Bad Companies and Make Good Companies Great* (1996): ix.
36. Syles, L. & Smith, C., *The Rise of the Rogue Executive: How Good Companies Go Bad and How To Stop the Destruction* (2006): 222.
37. Menkes, J., *Executive Intelligence: What All Great Leaders Have* (2005): 1.
38. Simon, G., *In Sheep's Clothing: Understanding and Dealing with Manipulative People* (2010): 44.
39. Denison, D. and Mishra, A., Toward a Theory of Organizational Culture and Effectiveness. *Organizational Science* (1995).
40. Denison, D. and Mishra, A., Toward a Theory of Organizational Culture and Effectiveness. *Organizational Science* (1995).
41. Senge, P., *The Fifth Discipline: The Art and Practice of the Learning Organization* (2006): 320.
42. Deutschman, A., Is Your Boss a Psychopath? *Fast Company* (2005, July): 47.
43. Deutschman, A., Is Your Boss a Psychopath? *Fast Company* (2005, July): 47.

44. Hogan, R., & Kaiser, R., What We Know About Leadership. *Review of General Psychology* (2005): 170.
45. Squigna, J. & Squigna, S., *Of Pathics and Evil* (2009).
46. Stout, M., *The Sociopath Next Door* (2005).
47. Ronson, J., *The Psychopath Test: A Journey Through the Madness Industry* (2011).
48. Senge, P., *The Fifth Discipline: The Art and Practice of the Learning Organization* (2006).
49. Babiak, P. & Hare R, *SnakesIn Suits: When Psychopaths Go to Work* (2006): 103.
50. MIPS Revised Marketing Brochure: *Millon Index of Personality Styles – Revised* (2013): 1.
51. Millon, T. & Bloom, C., *The Millon Inventories: A Practicioner's Guide to Personalized Clinical Assessment* (2nd Edition, 2008): 647.
52. Millon, T. & Bloom, C., *The Millon Inventories: A Practicioner's Guide to Personalized Clinical Assessment* (2nd Edition, 2008): 647.
53. Northouse, P., *Leadership: Theory and Practice* (5th Edition, 2010): 173.
54. Branden, N., *The Six Pillars of Self-Esteem* (1994): 4.
55. Goleman, D., *Emotional Intelligence*.(1995): 44.
56. Kouzes, J. & Posner, B., *The Leadership Challenge* (4th Edition, 2007).

57. Millon, T., Grossman, S., Millon, C., Meagher, S. & Ramnath, R., *Personality Disorders In Modern Life* (2nd Edition, 2004): 50.
58. Hein Online cited by Sprague, R., Googling Job Applicants: Incorporating Personal Information Into Hiring Decisions. *The Labor Lawyer* (2008): 21.
59. Hankin, R., *Navigating the Legal Minefields of Private Investigation* (2009): iv.
60. Nadell, B., *Sleuthing 101: Background Checks and the Law* (2004); 14.
61. Nadell, B., *Sleuthing 101: Background Checks and the Law* (2004); 148.
62. Sprague, R., Googling Job Applicants: Incorporating Personal Information Into Hiring Decisions. *The Labor Lawyer* (2008): 20.
63. Levmore, S. & Nussbaum, M., *The Offensive Internet: Speech, Privacy, and Reputation* (2010): 1.
64. Curtis, G., *The Law of Cybercrimes and Their Investigations* (2012): 3.
65. Determann, L. & Sprague, R., Intrusive Monitoring: Employee Privacy Expectations are Reasonable in Europe, Destroyed in the United States. *Berkeley Technology Law Journal* (2011); 986.
66. McLean, D., *Privacy and Its Invasion*. (1995): 5.
67. McLean, D., *Privacy and Its Invasion*. (1995): 5.

68. Hankin, R., *Navigating the Legal Minefields of Private Investigation* (2009): 46.
69. Hankin, R., *Navigating the Legal Minefields of Private Investigation* (2009): 46.
70. Hankin, R., *Navigating the Legal Minefields of Private Investigation* (2009).
71. Nissenbaum, H., *Privacy In Context: Technology, Policy, and the Integrity of Social Life*. (2010): 19.
72. Nissenbaum, H., *Privacy In Context: Technology, Policy, and the Integrity of Social Life* (2010): 19.
73. Levmore, S. & Nussbaum, M., *The Offensive Internet: Speech, Privacy, and Reputation* (2010): 237.
74. Andrews, L., *I Know Who You Are and I Saw What You Did: Social Networks and the Death of Privacy* (2011).
75. Nissenbaum, H., *Privacy In Context: Technology, Policy, and the Integrity of Social Life* (2010): 51.
76. Andrews, L., *I Know Who You Are and I Saw What You Did: Social Networks and the Death of Privacy* (2011): 3.
77. Andrews, L., *I Know Who You Are and I Saw What You Did: Social Networks and the Death of Privacy* (2011): 46.
78. Nissenbaum, H., *Privacy In Context: Technology, Policy, and the Integrity of Social Life* (2010): 101.

79. Zimmerman, M., *Interview Guide for Evaluating DSM-IV Psychiatric Disorders and the Mental Status Examination* (1994).

Bibliography

Allen, R. (2006). *The genealogy of bad management.* Unpublished research paper, Argosy University, Santa Ana, California.

Andrews, L. (2011). *I know who you are and I saw what you did: Social networks and the death of privacy.* New York, New York: Free Press.

Babiak, P. & Hare R. (2006). *Snakes in suits: When psychopaths go to work.* New York, New York: Harper Collins Publishers.

Barada, P. (2004). *Reference checking for everyone: What you need to know to protect yourself, your business, your family.* New York, New York: McGraw-Hill.

Branden, N. (1994). *The six pillars of self-esteem.* New York, New York: Bantam.

Brinkman, R. & Kirsches, R. (1994). *Dealing with people you can't stand: How to bring out the best in people at their worst.* New York, New York: McGraw-Hill.

Cashman, K. (2008). *Leadership from the inside out.* San Francisco, California: Barrett-Koehler Publishers.

Curtis, G. (2012). *The law of cybercrimes and their investigations.* Boca Raton, Florida: CROC Press.

Denison, D., Janovics, J., Young, J., Cho, H. (2006, January). *Diagnosing organizational cultures: Validating a model and method.* International Institute for Management Development.

Determann, L. & Sprague, R. (2011). Intrusive monitoring: Employee privacy expectations are reasonable in Europe, destroyed in the United States. *Berkeley Technology Law Journal 26*(979), 979-1036.

Deutschman, A. (2005, July). Is your boss a psychopath? *Fast Company, 96*, 46-51.

Dickerson, D. (2008). Background checks in the university admissions process: An overview of legal and policy considerations. *Journal of College and University Law 34*(2), 419-506.

Dickson, C. (2013, June). How to spot a sociopath (Hint: It could be you). *The Daily Beast*. Retrieved from www.thedailybeast.com/articles/2013/06/25/how-to-spot-a-sociopath-hint-it-could-be-you.html

DSM-IV-TRY (2000). *Diagnostic and statistical manual of mental disorders: Text revision* (4th ed.). Washington, DC: American Psychiatric Association.

DSM-5 (2013). *Diagnostic and statistical manual of mental disorder* (5th ed.). Washington, DC: American Psychiatric Association.

Dunlap, A. (1996). *Mean business: How I save bad companies and make good companies great*. New York: Random House.

Feinman, J. (2000). *Law 101*. New York, New York: Oxford University Press.

Goleman, D. (1995). E*motional intelligence*. New York, New York: Bantam.

Goleman, D. (2006). *Working with emotional intelligence*. New York, New York: Bantam.

Hadnagy, C. & Wilson, P. (2011). *Social engineering: The art of human hacking*. Indianapolis, Indiana: Wiley Publishing.

Hankin, R. (2009). *Navigating the legal minefields of private investigation*. Flushing, New York: Loose-leaf Law Publications.

Hare, R. (1993). *Without conscience: The disturbing world of the psychopaths among us*. New York, New York: Guilford Press.

Hogan, R., & Kaiser, R. (2005). What we know about leadership. *Review of General Psychology, 9*(2), 169-180.

Kouzes, J. & Posner, B. (2007). *The leadership challenge* (4th ed.). San Francisco, California: John Wiley & Sons.

Levmore, S. & Nussbaum, M. (2010). *The offensive internet: Speech, privacy, and reputation*. Cambridge, Massachusetts: Harvard University Press.

McAleer, K. (2010). Sociopathy vs. psychopathy. *Psych Central*. Retrieved from http://blogs.psychcentral.com/forensic-focus/2010/07/sociopathy-vs-psychopathy/

McLean, D. (1995). *Privacy and its invasion*. Westport, Connecticut: Pager Publishers.

McMillan, J. & Schumacher, S. (2010). *Research in education: Evidence-based inquiry* (7th ed.). Upper Saddle River, New Jersey: Pearson.

Menkes, J. (2005). *Executive intelligence: What all great leaders have*. New York: Harper Collins.

Mental disorders in America. (2013). *National Institute of Mental Health*. Retrieved from http://www.nimh.nih.gov/health/publications/the-numbers-count-mental-disorders-in-america/index.shtml#Personality

Millon, T. & Bloom, C. (2008). *The Millon inventories: A practicioner's guide to personalized clinical assessment* (2nd ed.). New York, New York: The Guilford Press.

Millon, T., Grossman, S., Millon, C., Meagher, S. & Ramnath, R. (2004). *Personality disorders in modern life* (2nd ed.). Hoboken, New Jersey: John Wiley & Sons.

MIPS Revised (2013). Marketing brochure: Millon index of personality styles – revised. Retrieved from http://psychorp.pearsonassessments.com/HAIWEB/Cultures/en-us/Productdetail.htm?Pid=PAg506

Mizell, L. (1998). *Invasion of privacy*. New York, New York: The Berkley Publishing Group.

Nadell, B. (2004). *Sleuthing 101: Background checks and the law*. Chatsworth, California: Barry J. Nadell.

Namie, G. & Namie, R. (2003). *The bully at work: What you can do to stop the hurt and reclaim your dignity on the job.* Naperville, Illinois: Sourcebooks.

Nissenbaum, H. (2010). *Privacy in context: Technology, policy, and the integrity of social life.* Stanford, California: Stanford University Press.

Northouse, P. (2010). *Leadership: Theory and Practice* (5th ed.). Thousand Oaks, California: SAGE Publications.

Path (2001). As defined in *Webster's* (2nd ed.) *New College Dictionary.* Boston, Massachussetts: Houghton Mifflin Company.

Poor managers hurt productivity, morale, and worker engagement. (2005, May). *HR Focus, 82*(5), 8.

Pseudo (2001). As defined in *Webster's* (2nd ed.) *New College Dictionary.* Boston, Massachussetts: Houghton Mifflin Company.

Robbins, S. P. & Judge, T. A. (2010). *Essentials of organizational behavior* (10th ed.). Upper Saddle River, New Jersey: Pearson Prentice Hall.

Ronson, J. (2011). *The psychopath test: A journey through the madness industry.* New York, New York: Penguin Group.

Sayles, L. & Smith, C. (2006). *The rise of the rogue executive: How good companies go bad and how to stop the destruction.* Upper Saddle River, NJ: Prentice Hall.

Sankey, M. & Hetherington, C. (2010). *The manual to online public records: The researcher's tool to online resources of public records and public information* (1st ed.). Tempe, Arizona: BRB Publications.

Schein, E. H. (2004). *Organizational culture and leadership* (3rd ed.). San Francisco, California: John Wiley & Sons.

Schouten, R. & Silver, J. (2012). *Almost a psychopath: Do I (or does someone I know) have a problem with manipulation and lack of empathy?* Harvard University.

Senge, P. (2006). *The fifth discipline: The art and practice of the learning organization.* New York, New York: Doubleday.

Senge, P., Kleiner, A., Roberts, C., Ross, R., Roth, G. & Smith, B. (1999). *The dance of change: A fifth discipline fieldbook for mastering the challenges of learning organizations.* New York, New York: Doubleday.

Shafritz, J. & Ott, J. (1996). *Classics of organizational theory.* Orlando, Florida: Harcourt Brace & Company.

Shaker, J. (2009). *Pre-employment screening methods: How much do you really want to know?* Seattle, Washington: Ryan, Swanson & Cleveland, PLLC.

Simon, G. (2010). *In sheep's clothing: Understanding and dealing with manipulative people.* Little Rock, Arakansas: Parkhurst Brothers Publishers.

Sprague, R. (2008). Googling job applicants: Incorporating personal information into hiring decisions. *The Labor Lawyer, 23*(19), 19-40.

Squigna, J. & Squigna, S. (2009). *Of pathics and evil.* Bloomington, Indiana: iUniverse Books.

Stout, M. (2005). *The sociopath next door.* New York, New York: Random House.

Thiroux, J. P. & Krasemann, K. W. (2009). *Ethics: Theory and practice* (10th ed.). Upper Saddle River, New Jersey: Prentice Hall.

Walsh, A., & Wu, H.H. (2008). *Differentiating antisocial personality disorder, psychopathy, and sociopathy: Evolutionary, genetic, neurological, and sociological considerations.* Criminal Justice Studies.

Zimmerman, M. (1994). *Interview guide for evaluating DSM-IV psychiatric disorders and the mental status examination.* East Greenwich, Rhode Island: Psych Products Press.

www.ingramcontent.com/pod-product-compliance
Lightning Source LLC
Chambersburg PA
CBHW051526170526
45165CB00002B/631